The Path from Backpack to Briefcase:

A Parents' Guide

The Path

From Backpack to Briefcase:

A Parents' Guide

Mr. R. William Holland PhD
The Right Job Guy

June, 2014

ISBN 10: 1497346010
ISBN 13: 9781497346017

Library of Congress Control Number: 2014905096
CreateSpace Independent Publishing Platform
North Charleston, South Carolina

A Look Inside...

"Parents do not want to see the dreams of their children die. That's why they have skin in the game like no other.

Getting your student prepared for an uncertain world is your job. And you cannot outsource it to others to manage—not to on-campus career services advisors, faculty, or newly developed bridge programs designed to do what colleges have not.

Eventually your children will grow to adulthood. But you will never outgrow your status as a parent. Thanks for coming aboard. The path from backpack to briefcase is before you."

Contents

Preface 1

"If Only I Knew Then..." 9

A Familiar Family Saga 10

Not Your Father's Job Market 16

A Book for Parents/Grandparents: Are you serious? 23

Five Reasons You Need to be Involved 27

The P-A-T-H: A More Detailed View 34

P=Parent/Student Partnership 36

How to talk so your kids will listen 38

Five things to talk about 43

Five golden rules for effective parent counseling 60

A= Achieving Academic And Career Success 65

A student's personal platform is important but... 74

Hard work hasn't gone out of style 81

Neither has focus 84

T=Treating College As A Four-Year Job Search 87

A visit that remains important: 88

How to tell if your school takes career readiness seriously 92

Is your career services center is up to snuff: 98

Skills employers want to see 102

Skill development made easy 112

Extra skill development tips 113

H=Hear To Be Heard 116

    10 tips for survival. 120

    Beyond survival. 123

    Networking: Are you serious? 126

    I know they can tweet, but can they communicate?. 131

Boomerang KIDS: A Family Saga Revisited. 133

    The end game 135

    Guidelines for handling boomerang kids. 139

Epilogue. 147

    Late bloomers et al. 147

Appendices

    Ways to Pay for college. 157

    Traditionally Underserved kids. 163

    The For-Profit Controversy 167

Index. 177

Preface

This book is a discussion about what parents can do to make sure their college-aged kids gain traction in the job market and their career of choice at graduation. Parents are worried. They should be because the requirements for job market participation have changed along with it takes to achieve career survival and prosperity.

Earlier in my career I was chief human resources officer for the business process management division of a major consulting firm. The name was a euphemism for outsourcing. And the efficiencies and money making potential were easy to understand.

A few years later I took another executive position with one of the world's largest career transition firms. "Career transition" is a euphemism for outplacement. We specialized in helping outsourced and otherwise terminated employees regain traction in the job market. The irony of the two positions was not lost. One job was a major source of worker displacement, the other, a means of worker reinstatement.

In both jobs I dealt with people who were apprehensive about the future. But in many cases it wasn't theirs; rather, it was that of their children. They wanted to know what to do to make sure their kids would do well in what was obviously a new job market—one where workers were in competition with one another on a global basis and a college degree didn't guarantee what it once did.

That's when the idea for this book was born. I was able to draw on my experiences as a college professor and business executive to create a book informed by both worlds. Since then, the need for this work has mushroomed. Over 94 percent of parents with children seventeen years and younger say they intend to send their kids to college because it is necessary to get ahead. This has happened at a time when college cost more and delivers less than at any time in our history. Parents want to know why and what they can do about it. That's why this book now exists. It is the only one I know that responds to the specific needs of parents—what they need to do before their student goes off to college; the guidance parents can provide while the kids are in college; and how to help them once they graduate.

As it turns out, parents can do a lot. You will be pleased to know there are not only numerous tips on what parents should do but also insight on how to do it. There is only one requirement: Get started now. You will find that it is a lot easier than waiting until later.

Explanation of Terms:

<u>Student rather than child:</u> A friend who read parts of the manuscript objected to my use of "student" rather than "child" or "kid." "That's no student," she objected, "that's my child." I understand her point of view. I also understand that students will want to read this book as well. Why wouldn't they? It is a road map to high-prestige jobs and successful careers. They will for sure object to terms like "child" and "kid." I don't blame them. With apologies to mothers everywhere, I have decided to stick mostly with "student."

<u>Companies:</u> The term is intended to represent all organizations that employ recent college graduates, including government at various levels, other not-for-profits, and small and large public and private entities as well.

<u>Colleges and universities:</u> The terms are often used interchangeably.

How to Use This Book:

I have included a detailed table of contents that makes subjects of interest readily available on a just-in-time basis. If you are concerned that it is difficult to talk with your student, consult the section titled "How to talk so your kids will listen." Want to learn more about helping your student link college to career? Be sure to check out "Treating College as a Four-Year Job Search." If your son or daughter has already graduated and is living at home, the chapter on "Boomerang Kids" may be of particular interest.

Feel free to skip sections that are not of immediate interest and come back to them as your concerns evolve. Though the chapters are interdependent, subjects are treated separately as much as possible.

Additional resources are provided on a variety of topics at www.therightjobguy.com. There you can ask me directly or consult a forum of parents with interests and questions similar to yours.

Appendices:

Appendices have been added to cover more specialized interests. These include discussions about for-profit educational institutions, traditionally underserved populations, and how to pay for college. None is intended as comprehensive coverage. They give you additional things to think about and places to look for answers.

Special recognition goes to Gale and Richard Mendes, Dr. Pam Rambo, Terry and Lee Decker, Erin Decker-Simpson, Jess Womack, Bob and Barbara Holland, Kheri Holland Tillman, Todd and Carol Holland, Kathy Lewis, Al Woods, Sharon Wood-Dunn, Ruth Scott, Lissy Peace, Jaime and Keisha Holland, Kathryn Canavan my fellow

"Skullers" (Pam Rambo, Nancy Giere and Liz Garrett) and others too numerous to mention. Thanks to all of you for your wonderful and much needed support.

Most of all, thanks to Claudia.

Regards,

R. William (Bill) Holland, PhD
The Right Job Guy
Helping people navigate the path to
career survival and prosperity

The Path

From Backpack to Briefcase:

A Parent's Guide

"If Only I Knew Then…"

We all would like to know what buttons to push to make our kids successful. It would have been easy had we known that one hundred shares of McDonald's stock in 1965 would be worth $1.6 million today. Many of us would have settled for an early notification that by 2008, bottled water (much of it from the tap) would become more popular than soda. Instead, we remain among those who forever moan, "If only I knew then what I know now…"

How we choose to invest in our children's education has similarities. For example, we have known for a long time that getting the kids through college is the right investment strategy. It worked for returning GIs after World War II; for African Americans in the 1960s and '70s; and for women throughout the entire postwar period. The strategy was so successful that we believed upward mobility was a predictable outcome for nearly all that wanted it. "Go to college, get a job, and join the middle class" seemed as if it were an inevitable progression.

That changed. And we are back to guessing which investment strategy will yield the best results. Most families continue to bet that a college degree will deliver what it once did. However, some are beginning to see that times have changed and a more deliberate strategy is required.

But the difference between the McDonald's stocks you didn't buy and dollars you are about to or have already invested in your student's education is that the latter can have painfully negative economic consequences for family and student alike. As students graduate with large student loan debts and jobs that pay less than expected, far too many families are left with the same familiar moan, "If only I knew then what I know now..." Rather than take your chips off the table, our objective is to help you make a better investment—one designed to get your student on the path from backpack to briefcase.

To get started, here is a family you might know.

A Familiar Family Saga

Their master bedroom had become a sanctuary of a different sort. It was now a place where John and Cynthia Ford could make sure of not being overheard as they discussed concerns about their youngest child, John Jr., who had unexpectedly returned home after college because he could not afford to do otherwise.

At times they talked about inconveniences—those that come with another adult living in the house; how different this arrangement was from what had been expected; and concern about how long it would last. At other times the talk was about finances—assumptions made, risks taken, and financial exposure resulting from Jr.'s inability to find a professional job at graduation.

The bedroom was actually a renovation and substitute for the new house they had planned to buy but no longer could afford because the cost of sending John and his two sisters to college was greater than anticipated.

It still had everything they wanted. There was ample room for a king-sized bed, a sitting area, walk-in closet, bath with double sinks, spa tub, and separate shower. But rather than a place to read and relax, it became a sanctuary where high-anxiety subjects could be discussed without intrusion.

The bill for Jr.'s four years came to more than $195,000, most of which was financed through cosigned student loans, second mortgages, and retirement savings. The expectation was that Jr. would begin repayment at graduation until the student loans were retired—a tall order given that his only source of income was walking neighborhood dogs.

Total out-of-pocket expenses for all three kids came to more than $410,000 and still another mortgage to build the master bedroom. The housing bubble created by the Great Recession left them owing more on the house than it was worth. Depleted resources meant concerns about the quality of their lives in retirement. As such, they were in no position to take on extra debt should Jr. default.

The Fords needed the privacy of their bedroom to vent, worry, and do additional planning without letting on how concerned they were or having their son think he alone had let them down. Overhearing these conversations would add additional burden to an already heavy load.

Meanwhile, John Jr. had taken over the basement as a way of also getting privacy. He needed space. He didn't want his parents to overhear him laughing with friends about living in the basement apartment—a standing joke among college students, but hardly a laughing matter. It was an embarrassment with no end in sight and, at this time in life, an unnecessary insult. His inability to get traction in the job market could be the tipping point for the entire household.

Elements of this saga are undoubtedly familiar. Though college may not bankrupt your family, it has become a serious economic and emotional strain for families throughout the country. Millions of Americans at all income levels face a rising tide of common difficulty as they try to gain access to professional jobs and careers for themselves and their children. And it is not just here. It is happening elsewhere—China, India, Canada, and around the globe. [1]

The situation stems from a set of conditions in a world that seems to change more in a single year than in the twenty-five years preceding the millennium. At a time when a college credential is perceived as more necessary, the cost of a college degree in America has climbed faster than family income; student debt is at an all-time high; and finding a professional job at graduation has become increasingly difficult. As a result, students boomerang back home at historic rates because they cannot afford to live independent of Mom and Dad. According to the US Department of Labor, a record high 36 percent of eighteen- to thirty-one-year-olds live at home with their parents.

The Fords did what good parents are supposed to. They made sure their kids went to college—good schools they were proud of so as to earn college degrees they thought for sure would help them maintain a middle-class lifestyle. They now face the anxiety of financial insecurity and a son who cannot find his way in the job market.

The cost of college is taking a larger portion of annual family income—30 percent to attend public schools, 48 percent at for-profits, and a whopping 71 percent of income for private schools. Most American families are forced to borrow heavily to pay for college. And the inability to find jobs commensurate with expectations has led to a growing student loan delinquency problem.

"Recent college students," according to a *Huffington Post* article, "are defrauding on federal loans at the highest rate in nearly two decades." Thirty-nine million borrowers owe more than $1 trillion in federal student debt with an average debt load of $26,000 per borrower, up 43 percent since 2007. [2] In time, John and Cynthia will see that careful planning could have delivered more certain outcomes. They could have helped Jr. look ahead from the very beginning of his college years to better understand what the job market would require four years hence. That is (and this is a central message in the book), they could have given better guidance so that each of his undergraduate years were spent developing a stronger personal profile—a portfolio of attributes and experiences employers across a broad spectrum of employment opportunities would find attractive. Further, that same portfolio could form the basis of finding new employment as it became necessary.

But that's history. They want to know where to go from here. Fortunately, the answers are essentially the same whether the issues are addressed before college starts, while in progress, or even after graduation. It all has to do with gaining traction in a new job market and regaining it once slippage occurs. And parents especially need to know that dealing with these issues sooner rather than later is always best. It's easier and in most cases less expensive. And one of the best ways to accomplish that is for students to be purposive about college from the very beginning.

Being purposive does not necessarily mean picking a major right away. At least starting to think about one, however, is a good idea. Some students pick majors they think offer the best chances of postgraduate employment. Others go through college without giving the issue of employment much thought. As you will discover, a college major is important but in the end makes less difference than most people think. It's not so much what major someone has as it is what one learns to do with it by the time they graduate. Postgraduate employment in the professional job market requires forethought regardless of choice of major.

Edgar Bronfman, billionaire and former CEO of the Seagram Corporation, weighed in on the matter when he openly expressed a preference for those with a liberal arts background because of the "adaptability of the mind" a liberal arts degree promotes.[3] Everyone understands that technical competence is a good and necessary thing. Employers that require that you know how to read a balance sheet or program a computer need assurance that those skills are in evidence before you are hired. But by themselves, technical skills do not offer the kind of career success most look to have. There are plenty of people who are technically competent. The question becomes what other factors distinguish one candidate from the other?

In other words, pushing the "technical" competence button by itself is not enough. Besides, there are many jobs for which a particular technical competence is not required.

Today's college graduates must be prepared to face a new job market—one that demands more fully developed skills as compared to what they have traditionally needed. And the sooner parents and students understand, the sooner they can begin to navigate the path from backpack to briefcase successfully.

Not Your Father's Job Market

A new job market has emerged along with dramatic changes in what a college diploma by itself will do for anyone's career. At one time, if you had a college degree, you could land a well-paying professional job if you wanted one. The path forward was to finish college in order to reap the benefits.

Those who entered the job market before finishing were routinely encouraged to return, even though it might not have a material impact regarding on-the-job performance.

It was as if appearances were more important than performance.

That happened at a time when employers were committed to the retention of their professional employees. Management believed that the future of any company relied on its ability to attract and retain talent over the entire course of an employee's working life. To get a sense of how much times have changed, take a look at the following excerpt from a 1981 edition of the IBM employee handbook.

> *"In nearly 40 years, no person employed on a regular basis by IBM has lost as much as one hour of working time because of a layoff. When recessions come or there is a major product shift, some companies handle the work-force imbalances that result by letting people go. IBM hasn't done that and hopes never to have to. It is hardly a surprise that one of the main reasons people like to work for IBM is the company's all-out effort to maintain full employment."* [4]

It would be astonishing to find such a statement today. Contrast that to a report that in 2013, IBM laid off three thousand US-based workers while aggressively hiring in other parts of the world.[5] A larger view of the data shows a dramatically more exaggerated situation.

Biggest Corporate Lay-offs[6]

Biggest U.S. Corporate Lay-Offs of all time			
Rank	Company	Size	Date
1	IBM	60,000	July 1993
2	Sears	50,000	January 1993
3	Citi Group	50,000	November 2008
4	General Motors	47,000	February 2009
5	AT&T	40,000	January 1996
6	Ford	35,000	January 2002
7	Boeing	31,000	September 2001
8	Bank of America	30,000	September 2001
9	U.S. Postal Service	30,000	March 2010
10	Daimler Chrysler	26,000	January 2001
11	Hewlett-Packard	24,600	September 2008

IBM went from initial reluctance to leading the pack. And it was generally thought to have been necessary for the company's survival. The acceptance of layoffs by IBM as standard operating procedure completed one of the most dramatic employment paradigm shifts in nearly half a century. Its effects continue to boomerang throughout the professional job market and on to college campuses.

Employers face competition from companies that can produce the same quality of goods at a fraction of the cost. Consider that an MBA in India makes about $12,000 a year compared with $100,000 for a comparably experienced MBA in America.[7] Also consider that there are not as many jobs proportionately today that pay a middle-class wage. Many of yesterday's manufacturing jobs, for example, have disappeared. Modern factories no longer pay union wages, as the work can now be done in China, India, and elsewhere. Nor do these jobs require anywhere near the numbers of workers they once did.

New factories, as one humorist put it, employ two living things—"a man and a dog. The job of the man is to feed the dog and the job of the dog is to keep the man away from the machines." Though not quite that bad, modern manufacturing facilities have neither the wages nor numbers of jobs for a return to the good old days.

The situation is aggravated by technologies that facilitate our transition to a service economy. In their book *The Start Up of You*,[8] Reid Hoffman, LinkedIn cofounder, and coauthor Ben Casnocha make the startling observation that the fastest-growing companies in Silicon Valley (collectively about the size of Walmart at the time) did not employ enough people to fill Madison Square Garden. That's great news from the perspective of worker productivity—not so much if you are looking for a job.

Consumers worldwide are demanding better goods and services at cheaper prices and are willing to buy from any company located anywhere in the world. Companies more readily see their obligations to shareholders and employees rather than their country of origin. That means the production, distribution, and selling of goods and services takes place in an increasingly global economy.

Competition is global, and beating the competition demands more, not less education. But unlike the past, the skill-set implied by having earned a college degree is no longer sufficient. Companies are more careful about whom they hire and about where in the world they choose to establish production facilities. Getting hired at graduation into one of the relatively scarce well-paying jobs requires more than it did a few decades ago, and the job search process puts job seekers in competition with one another on a global basis.

Allie Grasgreen, writing for *Inside Higher Education*, made precisely that same point when she observed:

> *It's not just that jobs are more scarce, experts say, it's that employers' professional expectations for new hires have risen dramatically at least in part because the companies are doing less training and hand-holding of the people they bring in.*[9]

Relatively fewer jobs and a fiercely competitive global marketplace combine to create a new job market that is more competitive for our sons and daughters. At one time students could casually treat college as a way station between adolescence and adulthood and still get positive career results. The name of the game was to get a degree because it was viewed as an "indicator" of one's ability to learn and persist—highly desirable characteristics during a time when one's professional employment was expected to last a lifetime.

Students today graduate with the same expectations, but are likely to experience an occupational downgrade because they are unprepared to enter the new job market.

The employment prospects for college graduates changed as companies were forced to adjust to rapidly changing environments or lose business to other more agile competitors. And we are just beginning to understand the rippling effect these changes continue to have on an entire generation of parents and students as they try to navigate the path from backpack to briefcase and beyond.

Jobs are not as secure as they once were, and the process by which we look for work has changed. New hires need to hit the ground running. And that requires more than just having earned a college degree.

However, some credentials are in such high demand that they get the attention of employers without demonstration of additional capability. But the attention may not last long. Jobs move—often to countries where labor is cheaper. They also move toward emerging markets. For example, though engineering graduates sometimes find employment faster than others, recent evidence suggests they also get laid off at rates higher than other professions.[10] At one time the bias was toward retention rather than termination of professional employees. That flipped in the new job market. An offer of employment (written or unwritten) was practically a guarantee of a job. Most offer letters now contain carefully scripted clauses that allow employers to renege at will. Increased competition has forced companies to be pickier about whom they hire, when they hire them, and whom they retain.

If this sounds a little overwhelming, it is. The forces shaping the current job market are global and raise serious questions about what any of us can do to manage our individual circumstances. In truth, you and your student can do a lot. But it will take both of you acting with purpose and in concert earlier in the educational process.

Urging parents to be involved with their student during the college years is new advice. That is, the prevailing prejudice is for parents to step back and let go—to treat college as an opportunity for the kids to grow to adulthood. Some thought-leaders have even suggested that interference from parents at this time "is ruining an entire generation." The point of view taken here is that students need your advice and counsel now more than ever. Our aim is to facilitate a better understanding of what advice students need along with tips on how to best give it to them.

Along the way you will meet parents and students who perhaps have the same questions and issues as you. Their decisions and results provide guidelines for you to consider.

A Book for Parents/Grandparents: Are you serious?

The Path From Backpack to Briefcase is written specifically for parents. We have added grandparents for obvious reasons. Their advice and counsel can be critically important—perhaps if it is nothing more than making a copy of this book available. The cautions discussed throughout the book about offering tactful advice go doubly for grandparents. Most of them probably know that.

Students, educators, and others will also find it useful because of the focus on linkages between college and career. It also has concrete step-by-step details about how the linkages work and how to better understand them.

Parents are the single most influential group when it comes to helping their student enter today's professional job market at graduation. It is an issue that gets bigger by the day, with a corresponding growth of service offerings designed to get students from college to career. These can be expensive add-ons to a college education, but parents should not totally outsource these services to others.

This is not a denial of the critical roles others play. Rather, it is recognition that parents occupy a special place of influence at critical points in time. The truth is colleges and universities traditionally have not accepted vocational readiness as their responsibility. If you do not provide career guidance during these years or see to it that it is otherwise obtained, there is a good chance it won't be provided at all. Here is why.

College administrators have debated among themselves for decades about what students should get out of a college education. According to a recent survey, 62 percent of senior faculty and administrators believe "critical thinking" is the most important thing for students to learn. But that view was held by only 26 percent of surveyed adults. Further, 80 percent of adults believe that the education students receive at some colleges is not worth what they pay. [11]

There is little ambiguity, however, among parents about whether their kids should attend college or for what reason. Ninety-four percent of parents with seventeen-year-olds or younger say they want their child to attend college largely because they see college as necessary to get ahead in life.[12]

According to the National Association of Colleges and Employers (NACE), students largely agree with their parents, as 75 percent of high school seniors have consistently reported wanting to attend college for vocational reasons.

We are back to what button to push. Parents prefer for their kids to pick majors that will be in demand at graduation. Unfortunately for them, it doesn't always work that way. Nearly 41 percent of the 1.6 million bachelor degrees awarded in 2010 were in fields of study for which there was no simple translation between college major and available jobs. These included majors in communications, English, literature, liberal arts, psychology, history, ethnic studies, and others.

None of this is meant to imply that these are inappropriate majors for finding a job or launching a career. The vagaries of the job market are such that more attention should be given to what students need to accomplish while in college to land a good job and launch a career. And that's true for all majors.

At graduation, students are required to do a more precise translation between their academic major and a job search. Chances are there will be very little in their undergraduate experience that will have prepared them for the task—an acceptable state of affairs under the old paradigm because companies were willing to absorb the cost of training.

Twenty years later the expectation was that many college graduates would be in careers unanticipated when they were students. They could land professional jobs and figure their careers out on the fly. The inability to land a professional job at graduation has changed the career arc of millions of graduates.

The lack of clarity is particularly perplexing for incoming freshmen. They are likely to lose focus on why they are in college as well as on what their end game needs to be. They tend to busy themselves making new friends and basking in the joy of independent living away from Mom and Dad. Graduation seems a lifetime away. Parents know it is right around the corner, and their student's ability to compete in the professional job market at graduation will depend on how well they use this time to prepare.

The sooner students get started, the better. Yet many high school seniors and college freshmen are not ready to fully engage. That is where parents play an important and even decisive role. This is also when those who "hover" over their children are labeled as "helicopter parents"—overly meddlesome and a retardant to their child's eventual growth to adulthood.

Expect a different point of view here. The job market has changed along with what it takes to find one's way and establish a career. While there is little any of us can do to resolve the debate among college faculty and administrators, parents are uniquely positioned to manage their own sphere of influence. It is not a question of whether parents should be involved as their college-aged children begin prepping for careers, but rather how and where along the way. That necessitates knowing how the path from backpack to briefcase works and what is required for its navigation.

Parents are encouraged to use this book as a guide—an introduction to the buttons this generation will need to push to establish and maintain successful careers. To be perfectly clear, there are…

Five Reasons You Need to be Involved

1. **PERSPECTIVE:** College freshmen have a lot coming at them all at once, including independence away from Mom and Dad. No one is around to moderate behaviors that could be inconsistent with long-term career objectives or gaining professional employment. For some, the exposure to drugs and alcohol will be a temptation too great to resist. For others, it could be the excitement of participating in all-night exchanges with other students and, as a result, sleeping past classes the next day. Freshmen tend not to worry because graduation is a long way off. Parents have a different perspective because they know how quickly four years will slip away.

   Students are in the midst of enjoying new experiences. Parents want new experiences to link to jobs and careers. Eventually students will adopt the perspectives of their parents once they see well-paying jobs as desirable outcomes. The sooner they understand this, the better. That is when they can be relied on to take actions more consistent with effective career management.

The perspective of parents that students need to take college seriously is consistent with what they will hear from university administrators, faculty, and others. Parents are uniquely positioned to drive the point home.

2. **AN EARLY START:** The typical student doesn't think a lot about graduation and getting a job until sometime in his or her senior year. By then it is late, and he or she is at a distinct disadvantage compared with other students who understood earlier and took action to do something about it. What action? That has to do with a clear understanding of what employers are looking for in entry-level hires and purposively developing the kind of personal profile employers will find attractive. It is not necessary to become job ready at the expense of other desirable collegiate experiences. But it is not an either/or proposition and shouldn't be treated as such.

3. **JOB READINESS VERSUS CHOICE OF MAJOR:** "But Dad, I don't know what I want to be." Sound familiar? According to some reports, 80 percent of college-bound high school seniors have yet to choose

a major, and 50 percent of those who have change their majors, often more than once. [13]This is understandable because there are many choices, and deciding what to do seemingly for the balance of one's life is a daunting task for an eighteen year-old.

Knowing what to major in or having a sense of career direction can be effective motivation and guidance. But it is not a reality for most students. Fortunately, employers look for a common core of attributes that extend beyond academic preparation. These are identified in greater detail later. They are attributes that can be developed through extracurricular activities, internships, volunteer assignments, and academic work. They are the activities that give potential employers a hint of the kind of employee your student will make. And they are relevant across all professional job categories regardless of major. They can be developed as the student's career direction and major crystalizes. These attributes are important, easy to focus on, and relatively easy to develop. And they deserve parental attention.

What a student chooses to major in is still important, and several suggestions are offered in upcoming chapters to help with the task. Meanwhile, there are a number of things students can do to ready themselves for the job market even as they remain undecided about their academic major. The message for parents is to never allow indecision about the choice of a major or career direction to be an excuse for inaction. There are many things students can do to facilitate the decision-making process and simultaneously enhance their attractiveness to potential employers.

Does the choice of major affect earning potential? Yes! If your student wants to be paid like a petroleum engineer, he or she should study to be one while in college. But choosing a major is not the same as choosing between a professional position and a job waiting tables. You and your student can discover the range of possibilities associated with various majors and what is required to be competitive regardless of what major your student eventually opts for. A simple way to start the process is for parent and student to visit the campus career services center and ask "Who comes to campus to recruit students with the academic major I am most likely to have?"

You may wonder what to do if your student still does not have a major and/or is unsure about what it will be. Even undecided freshmen have a good sense of their own academic interest and general career direction. If nothing else, find out the kinds of professional jobs that are available to those with the kind of academic interest your student already has. Is your student likely to major in the hard sciences, the arts, or social sciences? If so, find out what companies/organizations come to campus to recruit those kinds of majors.

If your student still insists that he or she has no idea, ask about jobs for which a college major is relatively unimportant. Companies will list these positions as open "to all majors." They will also show flexibility by listing certain majors as "preferred" rather than "required."

4. **THE TRUTH ABOUT CAREER COUNSELING IN HIGHER EDUCATION:** Parents and students sometimes equate admission to a high-quality university with improved employment opportunity. Though there is some limited truth to this belief, the correlation is not strong enough for parents to relax. Students who graduate from low-prestige institutions end up with high-prestige positions and vice versa.

A survey of college recruiters published in the *Wall Street Journal* identified Penn State, Texas A&M, and the University of Illinois at the top of a list of twenty-five best schools for recruiting. Does a degree from any of these schools guarantee your student will land a well-paying professional job? Neither one's choice of major nor school attended is enough by itself for career success in the new job market.[14]

Even if your son or daughter has a major that is in relatively high demand, he or she will still need to compete against thousands of others with similar credentials. And competition among recent graduates will remain intense across the full spectrum of majors for the foreseeable future. Parents are often surprised to discover how difficult it is for their student to find solid employment even when they have one of the highly sought after degrees. Others are shocked to find how difficult it is to hang on to a good job even after being highly recruited.

One would hope that career readiness would be a high priority among colleges and universities. By and large it is not, as the ratio of students to professional career counselors on American campuses is a whopping 1,650 to 1. There are not enough of them to go around, and many have little or no work experience beyond the university.

It is unlikely that the ratio will improve, as recent surveys confirm that university presidents are near unanimous in their assessment that higher education already does a good job preparing students for the job market. In contrast, a 2012 survey conducted by *The Chronicle of Higher Education* and American Public Media's Marketplace noted that only 15 percent of business leaders agreed.

What about faculty? Faculty best perform the function of helping students satisfy academic requirements. They are not trained as vocational counselors.

Some colleges and universities have taken a more active interest in providing better career counseling and job search support. But for your student, it could be a matter of too little too late or not at all. It is far more reasonable for parents to take up the "career counseling" mantle.

5. **PARENTS HAVE SKIN IN THE GAME LIKE NO OTHER:** Remember scoffing at your parents' insistence that "this is going to hurt me more than you?" As a parent, you now know what they meant. Few things are more painful than watching your children lose self-confidence as they struggle to find a meaningful place in today's job market. Parents desperately want to help and are willing to do almost anything to ease their pain.

Parents do not want to see the dreams of their children die. That's why they have skin in the game like no other.

Getting your student prepared for an uncertain world is your job. And you cannot outsource it entirely to others to manage—not to on-campus career services advisors, faculty, or newly developed bridge programs designed to do what colleges have not.

Meanwhile, sending the kids to college has become accepted as an extension of one's overall parental responsibility. And since 1978, the cost of that responsibility has risen 1,120 percent, four times faster than the consumer price index. During that same period, family incomes have shrunk.[15]

Eventually your children will grow to adulthood. But you will never outgrow your status as a parent. Thanks for coming aboard. The path from backpack to briefcase is before you.

The P-A-T-H: A More Detailed View

The path has several components. For ease of presentation they are grouped into categories represented by each letter in the word PATH. The groupings are not equal either in length of discussion or in their importance to the reader. Spend time on things that are important to you and revisit what you skipped as your priorities evolve. The PATH has many challenges, and along the way you will learn how some people faced them.

Our path is made up as follows:

P= Parent/Student Partnership

A= Achieving Academic and Career Success

T= Treating College as a Four-Year Job Search

H= Hearing to be Heard

We have included a short epilogue titled "Late Bloomers et al." that ties the entire book together. Take a look.

Throughout the book we note that the rules governing the path from backpack to briefcase apply to all: students who have yet to become freshmen; those who have already started college; and even graduates living perhaps at home with their parents. The latter group is given its own chapter.

"The path to any destination seldom travels in a straight line. We sometimes go down the wrong road, we get lost, we turn back. Maybe it doesn't matter which road we embark on. Maybe what matters is that we embark."

–Barbara Hall

P=Parent/Student Partnership

Parents know the job market has changed. They read about it in newspapers, hear about it on TV, and most of all feel it in their personal lives. Their kids can't find good jobs the way they used to.

Even summer jobs that once seemed available for the asking are not as available as they once were. From 1948 to 1989, more than 50 percent of American kids had summer jobs. That began to decline in 1990, and by 2003, it was down to 42 percent. By 2008, 37 percent of kids had summer jobs, and today the rate hovers around 30 percent. [16]The Great Recession didn't help, but it didn't cause the decline either. And there is no evidence to suggest the availability of summer jobs will return to pre-1990 levels.

Those fortunate enough to find good jobs at graduation live in a world in which unemployment may be right around the corner. Best-selling author Barbara Ehrenreich referred to this as being "anxiously employed." The entire sequence from summer jobs while in high school to a college degree followed by a professional job at graduation doesn't work the way it used to. Today's college graduates are more likely to be underemployed. That is, it is common for them to have jobs that fail to measure up to expectations in both pay and prestige.

That's the bad news. The good news is that parents and students can take positive action to help improve the situation. We have already mentioned some of the steps you can take to move forward. Now is a good time to address the issue in greater detail.

The path to a brighter future for your student starts with the formation of a purposive partnership—one in which you provide direction and guidance. It is clearly an extension of your normal parenting responsibilities, but it is also different. Until now good parenting was part and parcel of your moral responsibility. It was something you did because you were supposed to. Your objectives now include a mercenary component. The aim is to make sure the investment you and your student are about to make in a college education pays a personal dividend. It competes with the prevailing belief that parents with college-aged kids ought to sit back, let go, and allow the kids to grow to adulthood. It also challenges the idea that education is sufficiently beneficial without further justification. But ask, what other institution can require its investors to pay huge sums of money without offering a report card on how the money is used or be held accountable for outcomes? The burden for getting positive career outcomes falls squarely on the shoulders of parents and students.

The parent-student partnership stands or falls on a model of two-way communication. And that is why we begin the discussion with how to talk so your kids will listen. It is easy to understand that if they do not listen, they will not hear you. The logical corollary is, "If you don't listen, they won't either."

How to talk so your kids will listen

The partnership we have in mind is one in which parents and students have equal standing but the distribution of benefits initially appears to be one-sided in the students' direction. For example, students should be made to feel they are being listened to even though you may feel they are not as willing to listen to you. That's because the partnership is, after all, about them and their career—not about you.

Remember, they have listened to you all their lives and have had to follow your lead as a normal part of the parent-child relationship. At one time you dictated when to eat, sleep, and wake up. That sequence also included what to wear, what school to attend, and possibly even whom to befriend.

They are now closer to adulthood than at any other time in their lives. Never mind that you continue to see signs of immaturity in how they act and think. The simple truth is you won't be around them as much going forward and won't be able to determine how they behave as much you once did.

There is a good chance a lot of this independence from you has already happened. Your "control" will be reduced to influence—or at least you hope so. It is a continuation of the stage where parents need to tune in before they get tuned out. And one of the most effective ways to accomplish that is to learn to be a good listener. That is, listening is the first step in effective communication.

Perhaps you already are a good listener. If so, forming this particular part of the partnership will be easier. But just in case, here are some things to consider as you begin/continue the process.

Learn how to talk so your teen will listen: And listen so your kids will talk. If that sounds like a good title for a book, it is. Adele Farber and Elaine Mazlish have put together an excellent collection of anecdotes and suggestions on the subject.[17]

This is not a book about the details of how to communicate with your teenager. But effective communication will greatly enhance your ability to get him or her from back-pack to briefcase. That's why we touch, if only briefly, on the subject here.

Constantly interrupting a discussion with your point of view and opinions will disrupt most conversations. Here is an experience a family shared about constant interruptions and their impact on family communications. Tom was concerned that Donnie, his teenage son, wouldn't sit still long enough to talk with him—at least not about the subject of his college ma-jor. This took Tom by surprise because he and Donnie had always been able to discuss a wide variety of other topics.

The time for college was rapidly approaching, and Tom wanted to get a better idea of his son's thoughts about a pos-sible major. At first Donnie seemed interested in engineer-ing but had begun to think about other possibilities. To Tom, engineering was a good idea, but he thought to him-self, "With my luck he'll pick art history."

Tom's wife, Jill, wasn't at all surprised at the difficulty the two men in her life were beginning to have as they strug-gled with their communications with one another. She sug-gested that they video the family as they discussed the topic and view the tape separately as time permitted.

Tom viewed his tape alone at the office the next day and quickly understood why Donnie was reluctant to talk. Tom had been so anxious to get his point of view across that he interrupted early and often. For him the discussion was more of a tussle between competing points of view rather than a mutual sharing of ideas. Everyone got a clear picture of what Tom wanted and dissenting opinions were not exactly welcomed.

Prior to viewing the video, Tom's thinking was that Donnie's eventual choice of major was important. "Engineers will always be in demand," he thought, "and besides, it will feel good to have another one in the family." He treated the discussion as an opportunity for him to get his point of view across rather than to get a better understanding of what was important to Donnie. That was a mistake, and the communications flow slowed to a trickle.

<u>Deal with what's important to them</u>. Teenagers sometimes worry about seemingly unimportant things. But if it is important to them, it is, by definition, important to you and deserves to be treated with respect. This is a time when teenagers want to be adults but may lack confidence. Being told or treated as if their concerns are unimportant can be a demeaning turnoff.

Nothing written here will make you an expert communicator. Our objective is to guide you away from some of the obvious land mines that dot the parent-to-student communications landscape.

Meanwhile, let's move forward with getting your student on a path that ends with greater professional employment opportunities at graduation. Though it is not 100 percent guaranteed, the chances are considerably improved.

Your partnership begins with an agreement to discuss five critically important issues—all of which are relevant to the task at hand but whose importance may change as you proceed. Know that the first discussion establishes a foundation for what is to come.

As much as possible, treat all the discussions as continuous journeys rather than as immediate destination points. The distance from backpack to briefcase can't be traveled in a single evening of conversation. It has to be treated as a step-by-step process. And your ability to be helpful throughout the entire journey will depend on the quality of steps taken at each turn. Show that you are willing to listen and are open to their point of view. When they see that, they will be more inclined to include you as they think through the many decisions they will have to make over the course of the next several years. In this sense, the process is as important as the destination.

In addition, getting to a good place is easier when the right questions are asked. You can more easily steer that part of the journey if you become an effective partner.

Robert Half, a pioneer in the field of employment, made the observation that "asking the right question takes as much skill as giving the right answer." One of your primary objectives as a parent-counselor should be to help your student ask and think through the right questions in a timely manner. It gets your student on the path and acts as guardrails to keep him or her there.

The questions/issues below do not represent the full range of questions and issues that need to be dealt with as your student prepares for college. Instead, they focus specifically on the foundational pillars of the linkages between college and career. Other issues will become important. Other questions will need to be asked. But these are topics that build on one another and as such are anchors for what comes next.

As you go through each discussion, you will see why they are best started now rather than after a crisis erupts. These can be delicate and are best handled in the absence of crisis. They become guardrails because they act as a reminder of what is important and form the basis for decision making while your student is away at school perhaps busy with other important tasks.

Five things to talk about

1. <u>**To attend or not to attend...and why**</u>: This is sometimes a forgotten topic among those who advise parents with college-aged kids. That's too bad because it is a relatively easy discussion to have, the outcome is reasonably predictable, and there is a high probability of parent/student agreement. As a result, it is

easier for you to listen and thereby gain extra credibility in the eyes of your student for being a good listener.

According to the National Association of Colleges and Employers (NACE), over 75 percent of high school seniors report they want to attend college. Furthermore, they want to attend for the very reasons their parents want them to—to land a good job after graduation. During the Great Repression that figure skyrocketed well into the eightieth percentile and may linger there for some time to come.

High school students are constantly reminded of the need to go to college to get ahead. Most embrace the idea and get excited about the prospect. This is a great time for you to enter into a conversation about their plans after high school. For them, it's an opportunity to share their dreams. For you, it's an extension of conversations you have had since before they were in grade school. It's about what they want to be when they grow up. The difference between then and now is that the actions they take bear more directly on the outcomes they expect to achieve in the near future. That alone makes the conversation important.

They are important for another reason. Students who are able to keep their reason for being in college front and center are less likely to get confused by conflicting demands on their time and interests as they go through the college experience. That is, they are less likely to become academically adrift.

Start perhaps by asking what their friends are saying about college and over time move the conversation to what they hope to get out of the experience. Be sure to listen to what they say. This is a time for them to talk. Pay particular attention to see if they say anything about college leading to better employment opportunities. But don't be alarmed if their reasons for going to college change from time to time or if they do not always link to career opportunities. At this stage, becoming an active listener and gaining the confidence of your teen can easily be more important than the answers he or she gives.

What if your student doesn't want to go? Sometimes students say that for its shock value. It could be their way of asserting independence or checking out how you react. Don't overreact.

But what if they really don't want to go? It is far better to find out now before either of you make major investments of time and money. A reluctant college attendee will be less likely to take full advantage of what college has to offer.

Terri Watt, a single mom, found that out the hard way. Josh, her only child, headed off to college concerned about being overmatched. He knew that to make something of himself, he needed to go to college. This is what he heard from peers, teachers, and college recruiters. He was bothered by his prospects for employment as "only" a high school graduate. So off he went.

Besides wanting to see her son succeed, Terri's motivation was to show the world she had successfully met the demands of being both Mom and Dad. Josh's acceptance to a reasonably competitive college was a confirming accomplishment. That he really wasn't sure he wanted to attend was a conversation neither wanted to have.

The first semester did not go well, but Josh remained in school and was in regular communication with his mom. Early in the second semester, things went from bad to worse, and the communication intervals with Terri lengthened.

One evening she packed an overnight bag and, as if by instinct, started the long drive to campus, unsure what she would do once she arrived. A text message sent to Josh while in route read: "On my way to campus to pick you up. Come home if you like—Love Mom."

Later that night she saw the following tweet: "Mom coming to take me home. Called just in time." Terri doesn't tell that story often, but when she does, her audience is usually polite enough not to ask for clarification.

The discussion about whether to attend is also important because it can be used to reinforce the linkages between college and career. Have the conversation before your student gets busy with his or her new college friends.

Since faculty and college administrators don't agree on what students should learn while in college, it is not surprising that confusion sets in—sometimes very quickly. At its extreme, researchers refer to this as being "academically adrift:" that is, moving through college with no particular academic purpose in mind. As we shall see, there can be serious job and career consequences.

Students who have a clear sense of why they are in college and who have it reinforced from home are less likely to become academically adrift. It's a discussion that forms the foundation for important follow-up discussions you will have with them throughout their time in college.

How easy it is to have the discussion will be influenced by many factors including your relationship, the maturity of the student, and your listening skills. The point is this: As they begin to see the linkages between college and career, the foundation for the next subject is more fully developed. If one purpose of attending college is to get a good job, what needs to take place while in college to make good jobs happen? Is it enough to just earn a degree? What else is required?

2. **How to make good jobs happen:** The idea of how one goes about making good jobs happen gets at an issue neither parents nor students may think to explore. And it forms the basis for specific actions that lead to job and career readiness at graduation.

   Another way to think about the issue is to ask about the kind of personal profiles, qualities, and experiences employers will look for in entry-level candidates. And what actions do students need to take while in college to develop them?

   Both of you can find out and put a plan in place so that by graduation your student will have developed a competitive entry-level profile. Involved parents increase the likelihood that their student will understand and pursue this line of reasoning. It is also helpful if as a parent you know where to look for the answers.

The campus career services center is a good place to start. Visit the center together. You will discover resources and programs designed to help students make career choices. They will also learn more about different aspects of the job search process. These are important, but they are not the main reason for your visit.

You are there to find out which companies come to campus (or specifically seek to interview) students from your university. Make sure you find companies that interview students whose academic profiles are similar to the one your student either has or will likely have. This gives you a good idea of the kinds of positions and pay levels available to students with similar credentials. If those jobs are unattractive, it is an early signal to your student to consider a different major or academic emphasis. That can be valuable information. It is better to find out now than at graduation.

We have said the visit is important even if your student is unsure about a major or career. That is now amended to read "the visit to the career services center is important *especially* if your student is unsure about what he or she wants for a major or career." It will help familiarize your student with the one campus resource whose mission is to be responsive to his or her career aspirations.

Make a visit to the career services center as early as possible—perhaps even before the freshman year begins. If left for another time, it is possible it will not happen until the senior year or later. By then, many of the good jobs for recent college graduates will be taken.

As a result of the visit, you will get firsthand information about programs including internships, workshops on resume writing, interviewing, and opportunities ("meet and greets") to visit with employers on an exploratory basis.

Ask how the career center communicates with students and whether those communications are also sent to parents. If they are not, ask to be included or otherwise figure out a way to learn about upcoming events and application deadlines. There is a good chance your student will be too busy doing other things to pay much attention. You are in a good position to remind them and make sure these events become part of your ongoing discussions about college and career.

At graduation there will be thousands of students with the same academic credentials as your student's competing for the same subset of entry-level jobs. The most competitive graduates (the ones who began the path from backpack to briefcase early) are those who not only met whatever academic requirements were asked for but who also distinguished themselves in other nonacademic areas. The subject is covered in greater detail in the section on treating college as a four-year job search.

3. **Choosing the right major:** The subject is intended to give students a useful process rather than necessarily an immediate answer. Once you help them learn the process, they will be better equipped to pursue it even as they are away at school and away from you. That is, they have a heightened sense of how to approach the issue and to do more than just worry about it.

It also puts you in a position of understanding what is involved so that you can provide help when needed. You can also establish your own checklist so as to recognize progress and record it as it happens.

Some students know exactly what they want to study and what career interest them most. If this is your student, there is no reason to spend much time on the subject. Students who know what they want to major in have a tremendous advantage over others because having made the choice gives them a sense of direction and purpose and less chance of being academically adrift.

They also have an opportunity to get work experience/internships even while in high school, which may improve their chances of admission to their college of choice. Colleges tend to prefer students who know what they want and are focused on getting it.

While in college they are also in a great position to find out what companies visit campus to recruit students with that major. If they don't like what they see, it is an early warning. Perhaps they should look at other majors. Don't be alarmed if they decide to change. It happens. The question about who comes to campus to recruit their major will need to be asked again. This time getting the answer should be easier because they have had practice.

Some students (most) are not so sure about what to major in or what jobs to pursue. Eventually they will need to make a choice. It is useful if they understand how to approach the issue and know what resources are available to help.

Even when a student only has a general career direction in mind, it makes choosing a major easier. If, for example, your student likes teaching, well-worn academic paths already exist. It's simply a matter of finding out what academic work is required for entry into the teaching profession. Remember, even if graduate school is in your student's future, he or she still should use the undergraduate years to develop other job-related skills.

The tendency, however, is for students to reverse the process. That is, they often end up with a major first and then try to discover what it qualifies them to do. The approach is more challenging but can be made to work. Here is how.

If your student is one of the many thousands who will graduate each year for whom there is no simple translation between college major and available job, be sure and help them treat college as a four-year job search. That is, help your student narrow the possibilities and prepare to apply for those jobs he or she is most interested in and qualified for. When students graduate and do not know what kind of job they want, it is unrealistic to expect an employer to figure it out for them.

There are hundreds of assessment tests designed to help students find an appropriate career path and associated majors. Many are available free of charge. Some require interpretation by a trained professional while others allow those being assessed to do the interpretation. The assessments can be accessed through your high school guidance office, campus career services center, state and federal governments, and generally online.

Private not-for-profit and for-profit services are also available. Many combine the college application and financial aid process with career coaching and precollege internships. Put "career assessment tests" in your computer's search engine and you will get a sense of their availability.

Assessments usually help students find the intersection between their interests, aptitude, values, and personal style. An attempt is made to match them with those jobs and careers for which they are best suited.

The process can be confusing and you are advised to get help from professionals, but don't off-load the process to them entirely. Stay involved. As students explore which majors to choose, they should be engaged in the topics below. This may spark an idea or two about career direction.

- Subjects in high school they were good at or particularly fond of
- Hobbies that might overlap with career opportunity
- Careers/jobs they could see themselves in
- What do the assessments tell them?

- Who are some people they admire and what do they do for a living?

It's okay if none of these conversations with your student end in a decision about which major to choose. It is unlikely they will. The process continues to be more important than the immediate end result. Having a comfortable place to have these discussions with your student will provide greater familiarity with the variables that come into play as the decision is ultimately made.

4. **How to choose the right college:** Picking the right college has become an annual rite of passage for millions of high school seniors. Traditional considerations include size, cost, admission standards, gender, handicap accommodations, campus sports, and many others. These variables continue to be important, and there are plenty of resources to help (see www.therightjobguy.com).

Our purpose is to cover issues that may not be covered elsewhere. As postgraduate employability becomes more problematic, the list of considerations when choosing a college needs to be expanded to include some unconventional topics. Don't ignore the conventional. But do include these.

UNCONVENTIONAL DISCUSSION TOPICS TO HELP CHOOSE THE RIGHT COLLEGE

- <u>Companies/organizations that visit campus to recruit:</u> We have mentioned this as one of the objectives for visiting the campus career services center. Those companies now need to be explored in depth. They are important because of their predisposition to recruit students from your university. They know what they are getting in the way of new talent and like what they see. That's why they choose to recruit there.

  But, you may wonder, is this a realistic exercise for a freshman who does not know what he or she wants for a major? With the help of parents, it can be. Take a small sample of recent graduates and have university officials help you find out what kinds of jobs, salaries, and academic backgrounds they have and what companies they now work for. The objective is to get a broad-brush idea of possibilities.

  Expand your list to include companies similar to the ones that recruit on campus but currently do not. There is a good chance they are looking for similarly credentialed candidates and could expand the pool of available jobs your student might be considered for at graduation.

The exercise is especially important for first-generation attendees. Consider the case of James Wilson, who was scheduled to become the first member of his family to attend college. He had neither the grades nor the money to get into the colleges with which he was most familiar. He had to find the perfect fit—a college he could gain admission to and one that would minimize his out-of-pocket costs. He found two and chose the one that offered a degree in sports management. It wasn't until his senior year that he discovered that the college did not have a career services center (he never knew to ask) nor did they have good employment contacts for his major.

· <u>Availability of internship and externship programs:</u> Schools are quick to brag about the availability of internships, but sometimes they do not have enough business relationships to satisfy demand. Be sure to ask about the numbers and proportion of students turned away each year, the application process, how opportunities are communicated, and suggestions they might have to make sure your student is included.

Internships are considered to be of major importance by employers. Many are unpaid. Worse yet, parents now pay as much as $10,000 to specialty companies that provide "meaningful" internship experiences. It is a savings of time and money if your university of choice is prepared to facilitate the internship process. Your student still needs to take advantage of whatever internship opportunities exist. And that most easily happens when he or she knows to inquire about them and apply in a timely manner. It's another reason for parents to be involved and diligent.

- Employment rates and pay levels of recent graduates in professional positions: Hopefully you and your student will have a chance to attend one of the many college nights in your area and visit with representatives from campuses of interest. If so, be sure to ask how last year's (or the year before) graduating class fared in the job market and where you can get additional information. It is unlikely that college representatives will have the data at their fingertips, but they should know where you can find it. Colleges for whom employment is a major focus will not only have the data available, they will even brag about it.

  Be aware of answers that dodge the question, such as, "Many of our graduates go on to graduate school." While that might be true, there are some who don't. And if your student ends up among them, it's a good idea to understand who recruits there.

- Student evaluation of career services center programs: Try to get more than summary data and numbers. Also look at written comments from students. The information may be online and available to everyone. Students at some universities assume responsibility for collecting and distributing the information as a service to the general public without the endorsement of the university.

- Availability of career counseling: All campus career services centers have assessments. Go beyond that and ask for the proportion of students who use the center, the existence of special distinguishing programs, and how the center rates as compared to those at comparable institutions.

5. **Mutual expectations:** Once you have started the discussions, use them to initiate future discussions. Agree, for example, that you will revisit them at least once or twice a year to check progress and answer any questions that may have come up in the interim. The objective is to make sure your student knows help is a phone call, e-mail, text message, Skype, tweet, or face-time session away.

   Keep the channels of communications open by making open communication a priority. Your discussions form a foundation both of you will eventually be happy to have established.

   Communication with young adults is not always easy. Things get in the way, including family history, their maturity level, and your own communication skills. Here are some golden rules to follow that will make it easier to be a more effective parent-counselor.

Five golden rules for effective parent counseling

1. **<u>Abandon "Command and Control" language and attitudes.</u>** CEOs of major corporations are being advised that command and control no longer works when communicating with this generation of employees. The old method, "Because I said so," of getting compliance has been dead for some time. And it will not work very well with students either. They are already, or shortly will be, full-fledged adults who will be more motivated by a true partnership approach. The conversations are about them and their careers. They are not about you, even though you have a proprietary interest. Parents are required to listen more than talk in order to hear what their kids are saying. They will be inclined to listen to you more if they know the discussion will be a two-way street where their point of view is respected. Since the two-way street has been one way so long in your direction, it will now likely feel to you as if it is one way in theirs.

2. **Beware of unintended accusations.** That happens when as a parent you hear your student say that he or she may major in, for example, sociology, and you ask "what kind of job can you get with a major in that?" Never mind that your student has finally found a subject about which he or she is intellectually curious, the question is really an accusation and not a smart move. The accusation is that a major in sociology isn't worth much and certainly can't be used to find employment.

   An alternative response would be to help find out who comes to campus to recruit sociology majors and what else they require for qualifications. That can be accomplished with another visit to the career services center. Rather than a liability, an undergraduate major in sociology can be positioned as an asset that opens the door to other possibilities. The exercise will allow your student to look at future opportunities and to consider other majors if what he or she sees is unattractive.

3. **Use open-ended versus closed-ended questions during your discussions.** Closed-ended questions can be answered with one-word "yes" or "no" responses. Open-ended questions require more. "How would we find out what possibilities exist for that major?"

"What kinds of jobs did last year's sociology majors get?"

There is no guarantee your son or daughter will respond positively to open-ended questions. The guarantee is on the other side. They almost for sure will take advantage of a closed-ended question to end the discussion or react negatively to an accusation that his or her major is not a good choice.

Open-ended questions also provide more opportunity for your student to express anxiety. Once he or she knows you are willing to have an open-ended discussion without being overly judgmental, conversations will come easier.

4. **<u>Controversial topics are not taboo.</u>** Don't confuse getting along and keeping the peace with doing the right thing. Recall the earlier discussion about John and Cynthia Ford. Well before John Jr. was ready to enter college, the Fords knew they were overextended financially. But, they chose not to share the information. They would have been better off to have faced the issues sooner rather than later. Instead, they supposedly did what they thought good parents ought to. Careful planning and open discussions with all their children about financial limitations

and opportunities would possibly have resulted in more positive outcomes.

Parents sometimes feel locked into college expenses they can't afford. Kids are more mature than we sometimes give them credit for. Be clear about what you can and cannot afford. They will appreciate the candor and likely be willing to accept more of the financial responsibility.

5. **Agreement is not always required.** In fact, agreement is seldom required, especially during the early years of these discussions. It will occur naturally as you reach mutual agreement on employment as an important outcome of a college education. Meanwhile, end conversations in ways that leave the door open for future discussions. "Those are some good ideas," "I learned a lot," or "I hadn't quite thought about it that way" are useful phrases that leave egos intact and doors open.

Are there other rules you should follow? Absolutely! It is not our objective to make you an expert career counselor. It is to provide useful guidelines to follow to make you better than you would otherwise be. Do not hesitate to get outside help if you think it is warranted.

As you can see, forming a partnership can be an intricate process. Getting from backpack to briefcase is different from what has gone before. But at least you are positioned to embark. At this point, that's what truly matters.

Our next topic is about the rudiments of achieving academic and career success. It is the "A" on our PATH and deals with the issue of upward mobility in American society. Do those on top of the socio-economic pile simply stay there generation after generation? Is upward mobility really possible? Are your kids downwardly mobile? And what influence do parents really have?

You can decide. Our belief is that individuals can have a substantial impact on their own economic well-being even when the cards are "stacked" against them—if they know how. Further, those who come from positions of relative privilege need to be vigilant. Downward mobility is one or two job losses away. Parents can help stave that off—if they know how. The upcoming discussion is about how.

Understanding how to achieve and sustain academic and career success has value in getting from backpack to briefcase and is offered for that purpose.

A=<u>A</u>chieving Academic and Career Success

Much has been written about what it takes to succeed. The subject is included here because a lot of what is available is conflicting information that makes it difficult to come to sound conclusions or take appropriate action. It is, among other things, a question about how to use macro data intended for purposes of making public policy for individual decision-making.

Many economists, for example, insist that the odds are stacked in favor of the wealthy at the expense of the poor. Meanwhile, parents at all income levels show a persistent optimism when it comes to their own kids. No matter what they themselves have or have not achieved, parents continue to push their kids to do well. Regardless of the past, they act as if the fate of their children can be greatly influenced by whatever parents and students do next.

Kate Hollis felt that way and was inspired by the slogan "Yes we can" that President Obama used during his campaign. She listened when college faculty and administrators observed that college graduates earn more than their high school counterparts. Everything she could get her hands on reinforced how important education was to one's career chances. It was information that was presented as if what individuals do matters.

Kate, like most parents, believed the future could be greatly influenced by individual action and that a college degree is worth the cost at almost any price. Her faith was shaken by the experience of her daughter, Deborah, who a year after graduation was unable to find a job other than waitressing at a local restaurant.

"It must be the recession," they convinced themselves. And some of Debbie's lack of traction in the job market could be attributed to a bad economy. That's why they were willing to consider graduate school, which meant more expenses for Mom and more student debt for Deborah.

Their thinking had merit. According to a study by the Center on Education and the Workforce at Georgetown University, "a doctoral degree-holder will earn $3.3 million over a lifetime compared to $2.3 million for a college graduate and $1.3 million for those with a high school diploma." [18]

More education could mean greater earning potential. They were anxious to make those numbers a reality but stopped short when they learned of a friend's plight—seven years to finish her doctorate with a cumulative student debt of almost $100,000. After two years of looking she had not found work anywhere close to her initial expectations.

Kate and Debbie's thinking was flawed in part because they did not understand the specifics of how educational achievement links to job opportunity. Any university could show them how to meet certain academic requirements. But more would be required to achieve career success. Let's take a look at the job market from the perspective of employers.

Company executives complain of being unable to fill open positions because so few applicants have the appropriate skill-sets. And it's the soft skills that are most often the problem. It is not so much what someone majors in or the level of education they eventually attain. What's most important is what they learn to do with whatever degree they have. Further, this is true whether one has a GED or PhD.

Once it is determined whether new graduates have an appropriate level of technical expertise, it is about whether they are able to contribute. That is, have they learned how to be a good team member? Can they communicate effectively? Have they shown the required level of leadership? Applicants for employment who cannot demonstrate an ability to contribute will likely be greeted with a cold shoulder as they try to enter the new job market.

In part, it goes back to the lack of agreement among faculty, administrators, and others about what students should get out of a college education. There is virtually no focus on employability or life skills beyond academic accomplishment. And the results are beginning to show.

At one time a college degree was a distinguishing accomplishment and a ticket to upward mobility. It now costs more and delivers less than perhaps at any time in recent history. Today's college degree may be yesterday's high school diploma. [19]

And this has happened at a time when college is more accessible than ever to the average American. Upward mobility has become more complicated and simplified at the same time—more readily available but not necessarily accompanied by positive career results. No wonder parents and students are confused.

Economist Tom Friedman helped clarify the situation when he observed "average is over." By that he meant that at one time it was okay to be average. A reasonable wage was still possible. Average will no longer do today.

> *In the past, workers with average skills, doing an average job, could earn an average lifestyle. But, today, average is officially over. Being average just won't earn you what it used to.* [20]

Consider grade point average (GPA). A 3.5 GPA on a four-point scale no longer gets serious consideration for admission to most highly rated universities. Having "some college" but no degree puts you in limbo competing against others who have accomplished more. And having earned a college degree without demonstration of further accomplishment gets you treated as yesterday's high school graduate—very much considered average.

Friedman attributed the overall decline in the average person's ability to make a decent wage to technology and cheaper labor resulting from globalization. The global job market has an abundance of highly skilled people willing to work for shockingly low wages.

American college graduates also suffer from a confluence of additional circumstances—a lack of clarity about what they should learn while in college; adherence to an outdated paradigm about how a college degree is valued in the job market; and educational institutions that have not as yet devoted sufficient resources to the job readiness of those who pay the bills—students and parents.

Most agree that America needs to upgrade its work force by providing more people with greater access to post-secondary education and by upgrading the quality of education that students at all levels currently receive. That's difficult to accomplish when there is so little agreement on what students should learn or about how a college degree should impact their career chances.

The resulting confusion has contributed to a serious underutilization by students of the time spent while in college—a phenomenon referred to earlier as being "academically adrift" and reported on by researchers Richard Arum and Josipa Roksa in their 2010 book, *Academically Adrift: Limited Learning on College Campuses.*[21] In the book, they asked how much college students were really learning and what difference it made.

They tested, tracked, and retested 2,300 students from twenty-four universities over four years. At the end of two years, the authors concluded that students had learned little or nothing in the way of critical thinking, complex reasoning, and written communication—important skills needed to compete in today's job market.

Even if parents agreed with the 60 percent of faculty who say "critical thinking is the most important thing for students to learn," colleges and universities in the Arum and Roksa study failed even that test.

Students did not learn much while in college largely because they did not have to. They could "get by" without having to think much or work hard. Many earned college degrees that did not deliver what universities imply when they cite statistics about how much college graduates earn compared to others. It's a little like the Wizard of Oz, who insisted that what the Scarecrow really needed was a diploma, not a brain.

As additional evidence, the authors noted that 35 percent of students reported studying less than five hours per week, and 50 percent said they "didn't have a single course that required twenty pages of writing in their previous semester. Over all, the study found that there had been a 50 percent decline in the number of hours a student spends studying and preparing for classes from several decades ago."

The little studying that was done often occurred in inefficient groups (perhaps by that they meant study dates). And there was added pressure on professors to be less demanding because more demanding course requirements were often met with negative student evaluations.

We have no way of knowing if today's students actually learn less than those from a previous time. We do know that what they are learning now is not sufficient. And today's job market is offering its own brutal assessment of their ability to contribute.

It is hardly surprising that at graduation, the Arum and Roksa sample of students did not fare well in the job market.[22]

- Only sixty percent had full-time jobs.
- Thirty-six percent moved back home with family or relatives.

- Fifteen percent had debt of $60,000 or more.
- Two-thirds of the full-time job-holders were making less than $35,000.
- Forty-five percent were making less than $15,000.

Don't be lulled into believing these outcomes were solely the result of the Great Recession or that the job market will necessarily improve for your student as the economy rebounds. Today's students are handicapped because they have "little specific information about, or commitment to, a particular vision of the future" as they enter the university and later graduate. That is, they "drift" through college without a clear sense of purpose. Who can blame them? As freshmen, many are still not mature enough to understand. The model of accomplishment in their heads is that of getting a degree rather than of developing job-related skills.

There is a lot parents can do to change that. And *Backpack to Briefcase* makes it easier to connect college to career. That still doesn't make it easy. It requires effective parent-to-student communication skills, discussion topics that more directly link college to career, and the ability to sort out conflicting information. This chapter focuses on the latter.

Academic And Career Success Made Easier

How to link college to career is not something students hear very often from college faculty or administrators. Nor is it embedded in the institutional fabric of most universities. The task falls squarely on the shoulders of students and parents. As a parent, you accepted this responsibility when the kids were much younger. The responsibility now extends into college and beyond.

The students who opt to take their education and its linkages to the job market seriously can more easily be positioned to achieve academic and career success. There is growing evidence that the issue has gotten the attention of senior faculty and administrators. However, parents are advised to remain diligent. Career management is not something universities have traditionally been comfortable with, and much of the activity to date has been little more than window dressing.

Even when a university takes a leadership position, parents still have a major role to play. You will see why once we take a closer look at three interrelated variables: personal platform, one's willingness to work hard, and focus. Collectively they greatly influence academic and career success.

A student's personal platform is important but...

A student's personal platform is akin to what sociologists refer to as socioeconomic status and is a powerful influence in life. For convenience, the concept is more narrowly focused and renamed. Using it or its namesake to make personal decisions is tricky. Let's see why.

Becoming a more perfect parent is an objective shared by many. Clearly there is more agreement on the objective than on the methods for getting there. Consider, for example, the point of view of Steven Levitt and Stephen Dubner, authors of the *New York Times* best seller *Freakonomics*. In their chapter on "What makes a perfect parent" they made the observation that:

> ..."By the time most people pick up a parenting book, it is far too late. Most of the things that matter were decided long ago—who you are, whom you married, what kind of life you lead. If you are smart, hard working, well educated, well paid and married to someone equally fortunate, then your children are more likely to succeed. ...It isn't so much a matter of what you do as a parent. It's who you are." [23]

In other words, the parents' ability to influence their children's future is vested more in who the parents are rather than in what they do. Where does that leave parents who believe that what they do next is more important than what they have done in the past?

There is general agreement that a parent's socioeconomic status/personal platform greatly influences a child's life chances. Thankfully, that is not the end of the matter.

Let's take a closer look at what the data tells us and offer suggestions on what actions individuals might take as a consequence. Julia Isaacs of the Brookings

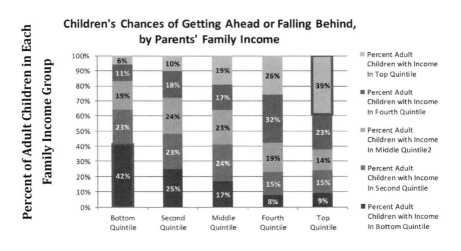

Children's Chances of Getting Ahead or Falling Behind, by Parents' Family Income

Institute studied the issue of family income across generations and sought to answer the following questions:

> *"... How are Americans doing today? Are they better off than their own parents were and how much does their eventual success depend on their family background?* [24]

The table from Isaacs' work is included for those who want to examine the data more closely, but it is not necessary to follow the discussion. It is a graphic display of "Children's Chances of Getting Ahead or Falling Behind by Parents' Income." And it absolutely supports Isaacs's conclusions that:

· All Americans do not have an equal shot at getting ahead, and one's chances are largely dependent on one's parents' economic position.
· Children born to parents (who earned the most) have the highest likelihood of attaining the top and children born to parents (who earned the least) have the highest likelihood of being on the bottom themselves.
· The chances of making it to the top of (income earners) decline steadily as one's parents' family income decreases.

But there are other conclusions supported by the data that provide insight and can help you help your children get to income levels they might value. For example, note that in the top group, 61 percent (23+14+15+9=61%) of the children in the next generation were downwardly mobile. That is, they did not earn as much as their parents. And 24 percent (15+9=24%) fell all the way to the bottom two levels of income.

At the other extreme, more than half (59 percent) of children whose parents were on the very bottom were upwardly mobile. That is, they made more than their parents a generation before.

At both extremes it could be argued that the kids had nowhere to go. Down in the case of kids from well-off families and up for kids among the relatively poor.[25]

It is also worth noting that middle-income groups two through four (low to high) experienced downward mobility at the rates of 25, 41 and 42 percent and upward mobility at the rates of 52, 36, and 26 percent respectively.

Whether this is better than or worse than other countries is of concern to social scientists and those who make public policy. Parents tend to have a different concern. They will appropriately note that there is a lot of upward and downward mobility in the society in general. Their interest is in what they can do to either keep their kids where they are or get them to where they might want to be. And there is reason to believe there are things individuals can do that will greatly influence the achievement of those objectives.

There is a growing debate in the country about vocational tracking. Its advocates argue that "college isn't for everyone" and cite various statistics that show correlations between parents' income, education, and college dropout rates. It might be a discussion worth having. But there can be no justification for taking those decisions out of the hands of individual parents and students.

It is curious, insists Angela Romans of the Annenberg Institute for School Reform at Brown University, that those who have this conversation are usually "talking about other people's kids, not theirs." [26]

Parents from all socioeconomic strata believe in the power of education. And the data suggest that it is a reasonable belief. It would be a dangerous and slippery slope were the conversation about access to higher education to be confined only to those who are currently most advantaged.

When students arrive at college, their personal platform is already established and cannot be changed. It is what it is. How that platform affects your child's future is not, however, locked in stone. And it is in that sense that "well-heeled" parents cannot assume their kids have it made or that the "not-so-well-heeled" are powerless.

One's personal platform makes it relatively easier or more difficult to do well. The other two variables, the willingness to work hard and focus, play major roles. Your job is to help your student understand what is at stake and lay out a path that at graduation ends with employment as a member of the professional work force.

Though the path we are discussing ends here, the struggle doesn't. From time to time we have referred to this as the path to career survival and prosperity. Survival involves the act of finding employment. Prosperity relates to the ability to find other employment again when necessary. It's all part of the new job market. Even those who find good work after graduation often are required to find it again, and again and again. It is a skill whose importance will continue to rise.

In today's job market it is psychologically healthier to view employment as a continuous process rather than an end result. Even though today's professional workers expect that their jobs will not last a lifetime, termination can still be a shocking and demoralizing event. It is important to understand these vagaries of the job market and be prepared whenever loss of employment happens.

That's the preparation that kept Jim Burke psychologically afloat at graduation when he came face-to-face with the new job market. Jim and his parents assumed they had made all the right decisions. They chose the right major and school—a BS and MS in engineering from Virginia Tech and Stanford University respectively. Though number one in his class as an undergraduate and with a highly prized graduate credential, Jim still lost his first four jobs in four years after college.

None of this was necessarily his fault, and he understands a lot better what it means to be anxiously employed. He was able to rebound successfully because the skills he developed while in college kept him going. Increasingly, employers get it. Tough things can happen to those who are otherwise qualified, and employers are not necessarily prejudiced against those who hold multiple positions over a short period of time. And sometimes, as in Jim's case, strong technical skills combined with an understanding of how to contribute and communicate continued to serve him well in tough times.

Jim's personal platform was strong. Still, he easily could have been downwardly mobile. He wasn't because he stayed the course and, as a result, brought the other two critically important variables into play—hard work and focus.

Hard work hasn't gone out of style

Do not underestimate the importance of hard work. Generally, students who work hard do better academically and get better jobs than those who do not. But how can that be when many employers say they do not bother to ask for or check the grades an applicant reports having earned?

Of course, some employers do check, and to have lied ends any chance of employment. The main purpose, though, of good grades is that they are an indication to both parents and students that they are learning—a reasonably important objective given that so many others go through college adrift. Plus there will come a time when circumstances dictate the need to put one's shoulder to the wheel and grind it out. It is a characteristic that can be learned and enhanced while in college.

Have the conversation with your student about the importance of taking pride in learning. Learning to persevere through difficult times and academic coursework develops skills that will be of value throughout life.

Students achieve better outcomes as they become anchored. That happens when they clearly understand why they are in college and how much work it will take to meet personal objectives.

Yes, college is a time for young people to grow to adulthood. But it is not a time for idleness or confusion about why they attend. Someone once observed that "hard work is the yeast that raises the dough." It is an observation that remains valid today.

Consider the following undergraduate majors: accounting, biology, business management, chemistry, geology, management information systems, and marketing. According to a report in the *Wall Street Journal*, over 1.2 million people with only a bachelor's degree in those majors had midcareer median salaries below that of a philosophy major's. We used the words "only" a bachelor's degree because the study sought to isolate the impact undergraduate degree attainment had on midcareer income levels, and therefore those who had graduate degrees were eliminated.[27]

The conclusion remains: career success and prosperity are available to those who work hard—yes, even those who majored in philosophy. Again, it is not so much what major one has as it is what one learns to do with it. There is obviously nothing wrong with majors that are in high demand. They make it easier to find good jobs right after college. But for a prosperous career, it is helpful to be willing to work hard and to have developed additional work-related skills during college.

You may wonder exactly what to say to your student to get him or her to work hard. That is covered in the section on treating college as a four-year job search. For now, be sure to mention that generally accepted student norms about study habits, easy courses, and large classes may be inconsistent with longer-term career objectives. It's the kind of message from parents that students fall back on at critical points in time. They may not always choose to do the right thing, but at least you have given them the benefit of knowing what you think the right thing is.

College athletic coaches are great believers that they can teach students to work hard. They routinely experience incoming freshmen who do not immediately understand the need to play a lot harder than what was required in high school. Coaches preach it from day one, but it takes time for each student to fully comprehend what is meant. Coaches keep working at it anyway using upper-class teammates and firsthand experiences on the field of play to drive the message home.

The vast majority of student athletes will not play professional sports. But a willingness to work hard before they perhaps understand fully what it means is important to the success of the team. That's why coaches, with support from the larger university, construct elaborate support mechanisms to help students work harder in the classroom and on the playing field. The hope is they will deliver at the highest possible level in the shortest amount of time.

There are no such mechanisms available to non-athletes. Yet in many respects they are expected to accomplish the same result. Your student's coach will likely be a faculty advisor who instructs him or her on how to meet the university's academic requirements and nothing else. The hard work of linking college to career is often left in limbo or to superficial programs that during orientation give only the appearance of having dealt with the issue of career management.

Your student is no different from a freshman athlete except that you may be the only coach available. The adjustment from high school to college and into the work force will take time. And what your student learns in the interim has important life lessons. Make sure your voice is available for him or her to listen to.

Neither has focus

"Would you please tell me which way I ought to go from here?" Alice

"That depends a good deal on where you want to get to." The Cat

"I don't much care where." Alice

"Then it doesn't matter which way you go." The Cat

FROM *ALICE IN WONDERLAND*

Focus gives hard work meaning. Drug dealers work hard, but their efforts do not have the same meaning as someone in pursuit of more legitimate work. When students focus on the linkages between college and career, education makes more sense. It helps them understand which way they ought to go, especially when facing competing options—to attend or not to attend—to study or not to study—to work hard or take easier, less meaningful classes.

One surefire way of getting through the educational maze is to have a focus that makes the same logical sense across many situations. When students learn to connect what they focus on with what they are trying to accomplish, another skill is added to their career management arsenal.

We mentioned earlier that successful job seekers first develop a laserlike focus on the objectives of employers before they even think about developing a resume. Some job seekers have a hard time understanding why this is the case and at the first suggestion of unemployment immediately sit down and update their resumes.

This is folly largely because it is the requirements of the job that give meaning to what you have accomplished, not vice versa. Employers want to interview applicants whose credentials speak specifically to what they are looking for when filling the job. And they only pursue applicants whose resumes most clearly demonstrate that. That's why it is best to first understand what an employer is trying to accomplish by filling the job in question. Applicants then have an opportunity to explain how their credentials fit those requirements. Credentials have meaning only in the context of the requirements of the job.

In this sense experienced job seekers understand that their resumes are not about them. They are about what employers want from them. And they construct their resumes accordingly.

The entire application process requires the same focus students are asked to develop while in college—an understanding of what employers are looking for and a focus on developing a personal profile that delivers it.

In summary, your student's personal platform (who you are, how much you make, who you married, and the advantages or disadvantages your kids get from that) influence life chances. But they do not determine whether your student has it made or is to be forever relegated to the bottom of the economic pile. Teaching kids to work hard and focus plays a hugely significant role going forward.

It is helpful for parents to understand how upward mobility works and to pass it along to their kids early in the college experience—often before students really care. The partnership and the rudiments of academic and career success are the first two steps along the PATH. We are now ready to turn attention to the specifics of treating college as a four-year job search.

T=Treating College As A Four-Year Job Search

Treating college as a four-year job search changes the dynamic of an undergraduate education. In a sense, it completes a century-long transformation in America of higher education from a public good to a private benefit. That is, the general population sees education from the perspective of what individuals can gain rather than as a generic good for the society as a whole.

Our path from backpack to briefcase began with the recommendation to have a parent-to-student discussion about why your student should attend college. It now turns to a visit to the campus career services center and four issues that affect your student's ability to personally gain from the college experience. They include: why a visit to the center remains important; how to tell if your college takes career readiness seriously; how to determine if your career services center is "up to snuff"; and how to develop job-ready skills by graduation.

A visit that remains important:

Context: At one time the career services office was probably referred to as the "placement center" because it was a coordinating hub where employees and students came together for interviews and job offers. That is, it was where students went to "get placed." Placement center professionals were largely college administrators who spent most of their working careers on campus. The lack of "real-world" work experience among their ranks continues as a concern.

Once an employer decided that a given campus was an appropriate place to recruit, little else was required from the university beyond the completion of some limited administrative duties. Faculty set the standards for graduation, college administrators kept the scorecard to determine who met the standards, and employers gladly accepted the college credential as the ticket of entry to their white- collar jobs. In many cases, the acquisition of specific job-related skills was left to company training programs.

But many of those programs have been drastically reduced or disappeared altogether as globalization and rapid changes in technology changed the competitive landscape in which companies operated. Tighter profit margins and greater competition meant companies could no longer afford to hire people who needed extensive training—especially if they were free to be pirated away by the competition at any time.

The name change to "career services" also shifted the burden of finding a job onto students. Career service offices evolved into places where students could go to get help if they wanted it. In most cases it is an elective activity and not part and parcel of the academic fabric of most institutions. That is, it doesn't automatically come with the territory.

Faculties have generally been reluctant to give academic credit for what they consider to be nonacademic course work. Thus a curious mismatch exists. Students attend college for vocational reasons. Yet their interests are seen as not having sufficient academic merit to warrant inclusion as part of the curriculum. Administrators appear more willing, but have yet to convince enough faculty members that career management deserves to be included as part of the academic curriculum required of all students.

The standoff has left parents and students holding the bag. They pay large sums for college because of what they assume a degree will do for their career ambitions. Meanwhile career pursuits remain as inappropriate inclusions in most college curricula.

Each year it comes as a surprise to many parents that students are essentially on their own when it comes to finding a job. They face declining attention from employers who once recruited them with enthusiasm. It used to be "go to college, get a job, and join the middle class." Today, far too many students attend college with those expectations and at graduation wonder, "Now that I have my degree, where is my career?"

<u>Still an important place to visit:</u> The career services center remains the one place on campus whose entire mission is to deliver against the career aspirations of parents and students alike. Make the visit. You will be glad you did.

When the kids go off to college, parents are in limbo. Maybe for the first time they do not have a clear idea of what their student is doing or with whom. As parents you hope they find time to do all the things they should. But you just don't know. You are not with them as much as you used to be and will not be present as they experience new things. You have to rely on what they choose to tell you and when they choose to tell it.

Plus, the university will tell students how well they are doing but they will not tell the parents. In some instances they are legally prohibited from doing so. In others it is easier not to engage. Universities have found that negotiating with individual parents is expensive, time consuming, and takes more resources than they can reasonably devote.

Incoming freshmen may be reluctant to visit the career center because they may not have the slightest idea about what they want for a major or a career. A visit to the center brings attention to their uncertainty.

Others may think a visit to the center is unnecessary because they already know where they are headed and have a good sense of how to get there. The problem is, of course, that they don't know what they don't know. And without the visit it is difficult to find out or discuss it.

By taking the initiative, you are assured of getting valuable firsthand information that otherwise may not be available. Visiting together also provides additional fodder for parent-student discussions.

Separate the visit from new student orientation: You will want one-on-one time that may not be available during orientation. And as you will soon see, your agenda is different and more detailed from what will be covered during orientation.

New student orientations have a slightly different purpose than your visit to the career services center. In fact, one of the clearest messages parents receive at orientation is when to leave campus. Some colleges even hold "parting" ceremonies designed to get parents off campus and away from students in a timely manner.

One university conducts the ceremony at the entrance to campus with parents on one side (outside) and students on the other (inside). Closing the gates sends a not so subtle message that it is time for parents to depart and leave the balance of what is to be accomplished to the "experts" in education. The attitude is a throwback to a time when positive career outcomes were more automatic and interference from "helicopter" parents was an unnecessary intrusion.

<u>Call ahead to make an appointment:</u> Career services people are some of the busiest on campus. By making an appointment you increase your chances of meeting with the center director or one of the professional staff. Be sure to explain that you and your student will attend together and that you are interested in understanding how the center works, what programs are available, and that you want their advice about how to take full advantage of what they have to offer.

Expect the face-to-face meeting to last between forty-five and sixty minutes and perhaps longer as you take time to browse.

How to tell if your school takes career readiness seriously:

When asked, college administrators invariably respond that they take career readiness seriously. It's just that some take it more seriously than others. How do you really now? Here are five indicators you can use to develop your own point of view.

1. **Resource allocation:** If you want to know what an institution values, take a look at how they allocate resources. If you want to know if they have been responsive to

increased awareness that career readiness is important, take a look at changes in resource allocation to career center programs over the past several years. That is, what percentage of the total university budget goes toward career readiness programs and how has that changed over, say, the past ten years? The information will not be easy to cull from the larger university budget. Ask anyway. Schools that have made changes will know what those changes are and will be able to quantify their efforts. It will also show they are at least beginning to take the issue seriously.

2. **Faculty endorsement:** We do not mean whether a member of the faculty speaks to parents about the subject of career readiness during orientation. We mean whether the subject has been imbedded into the academic curriculum and/or is part of the graduation requirements for all students.

    Consider the example of High Point University located in High Point, North Carolina. They offer a "Life Skills" course required of all freshmen. The rationale is as follows:

    "The harsh truth is that many companies today view new college grads as a hiring risk. Employers don't have the time, money, or wherewithal to

*teach them the practical skills they need to jump
the breach between liability and asset."*

The course includes, among other things, an emphasis on personal goal setting, leadership, fiscal literacy, and effective communication. One of its primary objectives is to prepare students for the transition from college to the work force. And it is embedded in the curriculum as a requirement for graduation. Lest there be any confusion about High Point's priorities, the course is taught by the president of the university.

3. **Career services recognition:** The National Association of Colleges and Employers (NACE) is a career services industry association of long standing that is dedicated to excellence in its field. Each year the association recognizes a relatively small number of individuals and campuses that have achieved outstanding results. One recent award went to Kate Brooks, executive director of career services at Wake Forest University. Her book, *You Majored in What? Your Path from Chaos to Career,* and Wake Forest's subsequent implementation of programs consistent with messages in the book got special recognition from NACE.

   Rather than list various winners here, make note of any special awards your center has received and ask whether they have applied for other special recognitions. By itself, it does not mean that the university as a whole takes career readiness seriously. But it is an indication that certain segments within the university community are trying. That's important.

4. **Efforts to redesign career services:** There is little evidence that individual institutions have either the will or talent to adequately address the issue. Faculties remain reluctant. Some administrators have gotten creative and have redesigned how services are delivered. This includes bringing more attention to the subject during new student orientation, making it easier to access center services, offering not-for-credit courses on various aspects of career management, and greater outreach to employers. These have been labeled "come-as-you-will" career centers that make center resources more available to students without truly rethinking the product.

   These efforts are important because they are indications that a certain energy exists among campus career service professionals aimed at improving service delivery. But until they succeed with enlisting faculty endorsement and getting a greater share of budget, they are largely window dressing. More aggressive efforts on other campuses give those students an undeniable advantage.

Demand for career readiness programs has continued to grow as the on-campus debate edges slowly along. Meanwhile, a number of for-profit bridge programs have sprung up designed to fill the college-to-career transition gap. A variety of models are used, including partnering with liberal arts colleges and employers; real-world learning opportunities for faculty, students, and businesses; and internship opportunities accessed through online billboards.[28] Initial results have been positive as they focus on practical on-the-job skills.

However, even these programs appear reluctant to reach out to parents, and some charge substantial fees, as much as $10,000.

5. **Partnering with parents:** There is a sad truth that many career service professionals know but hesitate to discuss. If students really got interested in career services, the center would quickly be overrun. They are careful not to generate too much demand because of limited resources. We suspect that's part of the reason career centers are not terribly aggressive when it comes to partnering with parents. Those that do are ahead of the game.

Parents make perfect partners. They believe in career planning and encourage students to pay attention. There is also the distinct possibility that parents would make more aggressive financial contributions to the university if the university were more aggressive in its pursuit of career-relevant experiences for students. But that doesn't happen, especially when the career services center is not well integrated into the administrative and academic fabric of the university.

New programs are popping up. There is one at The Ohio State University that works with parents and students to help both navigate the university landscape. At the University of Vermont, one such program focuses specifically on career services. And programs have gotten started at Northwestern and the University of Pennsylvania.

Not enough programs are yet available, and the those that focus specifically on empowering parents to become more effective career counselors remain small.

The career services landscape on college campuses needs to evolve more quickly. Whether it does or doesn't, parents need to commit to the career readiness of their kids.

Is your career services center is up to snuff:

It is too bad most parents never get a chance to interview the career center services center director from one of the top ten MBA schools. If they did, they would see how effective centers are run. You can tell they are different because they tend to keep their distance from career services in the rest of the university.

Top MBA programs have for years run their own shop and follow the business adage to "inspect what they expect." They expect their students to be recruited by some of the most prestigious employers in the world. It is a claim they back up with data collected every year on every graduating student.

There are ways to find out if the center that will service your student is up to snuff. It is an important thing for you to do. Your student's career may be riding on it.

7 WAYS TO TELL IF YOUR CAREER CENTER IS UP TO SNUFF

1. <u>Availability of career counseling tools:</u> Ask what assessment tools are available to help students make the right career choices. It is difficult to imagine a center without a wide array of tools because assessment is the lifeblood of career services professionals. The

question gets at whether or not follow-up requires someone trained to use particular instruments or if the assessments are self-directed. The latter instruments are usually less precise and require little or no financial investment by the university. They can still be useful. But their availability is hardly worth bragging about; nor are they an indication that the university has committed significant resources to career readiness.

Also get a sense of the numbers of students who use the center for that purpose. It is unrealistic to expect that a large percentage of the student population will have requested help. But it is a number that is easily tracked, and well-run centers have them readily available.

2. **Standard job support services:** Ask for descriptions of the standard programs available to students such as resume writing, cover letters, and preparing for interviews. These programs are usually offered each semester in workshops. Ask if students sometimes do not have access to them because they do not sign up in a timely manner or if the courses are filled to capacity. If so, it is an indication that the center is behind the times and has not put the courses online.

3. **How students rate the career services center:** Student evaluations are usually available to the general public. Before your meeting is scheduled, take a look at the most recent evaluations. Whether negative or positive, inquire about why the ratings are as they are. Familiarity with what students are saying is an indication senior staff is in touch with student opinion. Most well-run centers will have plans to improve even if the evaluations are mostly positive.

   If the ratings are not available, be sure to ask why. Don't settle for generalities. Awareness that the evaluations exist and the commitment to maintain or improve services demonstrate sensitivity to and awareness of the value of student feedback.

4. **Internship and externship programs:** Employers usually prefer that students have work experience in the way of one or two internships during college. Externships (programs that allow a student to shadow a professional for a day or two), though not as desirable, are reasonable substitutes.

   Find out if there are a sufficient number of opportunities to reasonably accommodate the number of interested students. On some campuses, there simply are not enough opportunities to go around, and perfectly qualified and interested students are left out.

5. **Career services for alumni:** Once your student graduates, he or she may need support from career services. The best indicator of whether support will be available is what is currently available to existing alumni. Some schools leave alumni matters strictly to the alumni association, whose primary objective is fund raising rather than career management. It is not enough to offer occasional support. Find out if there are formal programs in place and the numbers of alumni who take advantage.

   Besides, active and engaged alumni are additional contacts for networking support.

6. **Communication programs:** Well-run centers have more than newsletters available to communicate with students. They have communication programs with specific goals and objectives. Pay attention to how they refer to their communications with students. Nearly all career centers publish a calendar of events and notices of upcoming activities. This is your chance to make sure your student knows how and when the center expects to communicate with him or her and the center's objectives for doing so. Encourage your student to be aware of upcoming events and to attend when appropriate.

7. **Communication with parents:** Why parents feel as if they are the last to know is unclear. Perhaps it is because they are. Career centers do not usually send communications directed at students to parents. They should. Parents are perfect allies. They are interested, tend to pay attention, and will be better able to get the attention of their student.

Sometimes expense is used as an excuse. But most communications are online with no incremental costs associated with sending additional copies. Expense should not be a factor.

Direct parental involvement, however, will for sure increase individualized communications traffic and some added expense. But that's a good thing and worth budgeting for. Ask to be included on communications to students. It's worth a try.

Skills employers want to see

Because college should be treated as a four-year job search, it is an advantage to take a look at techniques experienced job seekers use to find employment. As the job market became more competitive, techniques changed. For example, job search counselors routinely advised clients to keep their resumes updated in the event of a sudden job loss. The idea was to always be ready so as to get back in the job market quickly. A well-written resume, the thinking was, could be circulated again after minor tweaks and appropriate updates to reflect additional job duties since the last time it was used.

In today's job market that is now bad advice. Before giving any thought to their resume, job seekers first need to determine exactly what an employer is looking to accomplish by filling a job in which they have interest. Resumes need to be written so as to emphasize what is of interest to the employer. That interest, in combination with an applicant's experiences, drives the content of a resume right down to the words used to describe work experiences.

When applicants fail to start with what an employer is looking for, they risk developing resumes that miss the target audience. Those are the ones that get tossed immediately into the wastebasket. In an online application process, the typical resume gets no more than a ten- to fifteen-second scan. There can be hundreds, even thousands of applicants for a single position. Employers cannot afford to take time and figure out which of an applicant's experiences are relevant to the job in question. That has to be demonstrated up front and right away.

Some job seekers have difficulty grasping the concept. To drive the point home, we tell them their resume is not about them. It's about what employers want from them. And the chances of being invited in for an interview are greatly enhanced if they can find out what the employer is interested in and reflect it on the resume.

How can someone find out what employers are looking for regarding a specific job vacancy? They find it in the position description accompanying the opening. Companies gladly communicate what they are looking for. Applicants need only take advantage by carefully reviewing the job requirements and responding appropriately.

That brings to mind an advantage college students have over experienced job seekers that is seldom discussed. Candidates with already existing work experience often need to retrofit what they have done to the requirements of a job opening. That is, they have to describe what they have done in creative ways. For example, if a company is looking for someone to be a project manager, an applicant could be a strong candidate even though he or she may not have held that specific title. How? The candidate may have had enough equivalent experience to qualify, but he or she will need to represent that background accordingly.

In other words, candidates have to play a hand (their existing job experience) that has already been dealt. In this respect experienced job seekers behave retroactively. College students, on the other hand, have a wonderful opportunity to be proactive. That is, they can look ahead to see what skills and experiences entry-level applicants will need and use their time in college to develop them. The sooner they get started the easier it will be. Both you and your student can find out what employers will be looking for when you visit the career services center. Here's how.

Based on your student's aptitude and interests, visit the campus career center and ask for copies of three kinds of position descriptions companies provide when they recruit on campus—jobs for which your student's college major is specified, others for which college majors are recommended, and positions open virtually to all majors. If, for example, your student wants to major in psychology, position descriptions that specify that major will tell you the range of employment possibilities available to undergraduate psychology majors.

You may wonder if this information loses its value when a student changes majors. Not as much as you might think. Though specific academic requirements may be substantially different (a major in petroleum engineering as compared with one in sociology, for example) the underlying nonacademic skill sets employers want to see could be very similar and applicable across a wide variety of entry-level opportunities.

An understanding of what employers want to see in applicants beginning the freshman year eliminates the surprises in the senior year that send students scurrying about in search of employment. The freshman year is also a good time to get an understanding about starting salaries and what the return might be on your educational dollars. For example, will your student make enough to live on his or her own and still pay down student loans?

Parents need to be available to bridge the information gap between the job market freshmen will inevitably encounter and what they might learn when left to their own devices. The three steps below will help you manage the meeting and get the information your student needs to determine the skills he or she needs to develop over the next four years.

Step #1: Start your meeting by asking, "Who visits campus to recruit students with academic credentials similar to those my student will likely have?" Speculation here is more important than accuracy. Be willing to examine various possibilities. It will help you discover important patterns of requirements that emerge for entry-level positions.

Employers will specify interest in at least one of three levels of academic preparation. The first refers to jobs for which a specific academic major is required. A student either has it or doesn't/will major in it or won't.

Companies also ask to see students with majors that are "preferred" but not required. The academic requirements are less stringent. Look for positions that may be of interest along with the preferred academic majors.

The final category consists of jobs that are "open to all or most majors." Employers are most interested in whether your student has graduated. All three categories of jobs will give you and your student a profile of available opportunities, job locations, and starting salaries. If nothing of interest is identified, it's a signal to begin looking for a different set of entry-level jobs with perhaps different academic requirements.

The next step is critical.

<u>Step #2: Ask for copies of position descriptions from companies/organizations of jobs in which there is a reasonable level of interest.</u> Those descriptions tell you precisely what companies are looking for in entry-level candidates. They are neither secret nor (as some center personnel insist) confidential. Companies cannot recruit without clear communications to students about what they are looking for. You simply are trying to find out ahead of time.

<u>Step #3: Identify and highlight all the key words employers use to describe their positions.</u> By the time you have reviewed ten to fifteen positions, you will begin to see patterns of requirements across job openings regardless of major. These are the skills employers look for students to have at graduation. Many are not, by and large, dependent on a specific college major.

If your student has not met the academic requirements specified for certain positions, there is little you can do. Be sure to identify positions that are available given the degree your student will earn.

Hopefully by graduation both of you know the full range of skills and experiences that will make your student competitive.

We have listed seven skills employers frequently ask for in recent college graduates. Still go through the exercise because it is good practice. You may discover additional skills unique to certain positions.

7 SKILLS EMPLOYERS WANT TO SEE

1. **COMMUNICATION:** Value that cannot be well communicated will likely go unnoticed. Never mind that your student does not like to write or is reluctant to speak in front of groups. Most people are like that. They need to develop those skills anyway. Human resources executives complain that applicants today display a shocking inability to do either. By learning these skills, your student will be ahead of the game.

2. **TEAMWORK:** Modern organizational structures are relatively flat and use fewer people. Employees have to work in teams (often self-directed) to get things done. Some Silicon Valley companies report evaluating team leaders at the end of every fiscal quarter because they cannot afford to wait longer periods to discover that things are not working out. Teamwork is a basic requirement of the new job

market. The advantage goes to those who can demonstrate they understand effective teamwork.

3. **DECISION MAKING/CRITICAL THINKING:** Modern organizations tend to be flatter and less bureaucratic. As such, it is easier for individual thought to make its way to decision makers. Now the insights of a single individual could save or make companies millions of dollars. Effective decision-making is a skill worth developing and learning to communicate.

4. **SELF-IMPROVEMENT:** An interview was abruptly ended when an applicant was asked about the "biggest mistake he had ever made." He responded, "I don't make mistakes." That's when the interview ended. Companies want employees who are self-aware and able to learn on the job.

5. **LEADERSHIP:** In response to the question "What leadership positions did you hold while in school?" another applicant said she chose to concentrate on her grades rather than run for elective office. She completely missed the point of the question. There are plenty of opportunities to show leadership in ways that do not involve elective office. Leadership is not necessarily the outcome of a popularity contest.

It is much more. College is an opportunity to develop a substantial understanding of the concept.

6. **HONESTY AND INTEGRITY:** The concept is so important for some companies that they test for it, especially in jobs where bonding is required. It is a great advantage when companies have a reputation for the honesty and integrity of its employees.

7. **PROBLEM SOLVING:** An often overlooked skill that is arguably the granddaddy of all. Successful enterprises first and foremost solve problems. It is a skill that usually brings all the other skills into play.

Are there other skills that are important? There are. That's one of the reasons you and your student should go through the exercise. Public-facing jobs, for example, may have a different emphasis on the skills required to succeed as compared to individual contributor positions.

Traditionalists sometimes have difficulty believing companies really value soft skills. They might be interested to know many companies no longer consider those skills as soft. Take Google, for example. About 50 percent of their roles are in technical positions, and technical skills are important. Beyond that, Google looks for the following hiring attributes: cognitive ability (not IQ), leadership (did you step in and help solve a problem when the situation called for it?), humility (the ability to embrace ideas that are not your own), and ownership.

If your student wants to work for Google, it will help mightily to understand what they are looking for and spend the undergraduate years developing those characteristics. If so, your student will also likely qualify for a number of other positions in other companies as well. An undergraduate engineering or computer science degree might help, but it won't suffice.[29]

You have reason to be confident that your student will be competitive if he or she can reasonably lay claim to substantive accomplishments in the seven skill areas we have identified.

Those skills become doubly significant when combined with specific academic requirements. What oil company couldn't use entry-level employees who are effective communicators, know how to work in teams, are good decision makers, and on and on? The same is true of employers looking to hire, for example, history majors. I think you get the point.

It is one thing to identify the skills and another to move forward with their development. How do you and your student go about developing these skills during the undergraduate years?

Skill development made easy

There are four primary arenas in college that provide a context for skill development. Students are always encouraged to participate in activities that pique their interest. But don't let interests alone be their guide. Help them be purposive about college activities. Have your student ask, "How can my activities this semester be used to develop job or career-related skills?"

The context for skill development includes: extracurricular activities (campus clubs), classes, internships, and volunteer work. All present opportunities for skill development for each of the seven skill areas and more. They can also be used in ways other than those listed below. Our purpose is to get you thinking rather than provide an exhaustive list.

Academic work (classes): There are a great many academic courses available that will help your student develop important skills that may not be part of the requirements for his or her major. Possibilities that come to mind include communication, creative writing, philosophy, logic, foreign languages, English composition, literature, presentation skills, and others. They are available for the choosing.

Also, do not overlook opportunities in required coursework. Generally, have your student approach his or her educational experience with purpose.

Extracurricular activities (campus clubs): Start with clubs that are sanctioned by the university. They tend to operate under guidelines that are helpful to students. Once your student gets his or her feet on the ground, branch out. Pick clubs with a particular skill development opportunity in mind. It will act as a rudder once activities begin.

Internships: Two internship experiences are better than one. Find out where the opportunities are and sign up early. Using an intern effectively is difficult, and many companies haven't mastered the art. Don't be dismayed. Tell your student to do what is asked (providing, of course, it is legal and ethical) and look for opportunities to make contributions that are worthy of inclusion on a resume. Just having had the experience is a feather in one's cap.

Volunteer assignments: These are available in the form of service to the larger community. Charitable organizations are always on the lookout for volunteers. It's a good way to build teamwork skills and the ability to influence without authority—an important skill that until now we have not mentioned. People who volunteer do so because they want to rather than have to. Interpersonal effectiveness depends on one's ability to influence without authority, one of the essential elements of effective teamwork.

Extra skill development tips

Don't confuse activity with accomplishment: This is a mistake experienced job seekers make all the time. They list jobs held and assume the accomplishments are self-evident.

Not true. The most successful job seekers find out what the employer is looking for and describe their accomplishments in that context.

The same tactic is appropriate for skill-development activities while in college. We already know the skills employers are looking for. The question becomes what was accomplished as they were developed? Activities without accomplishments have little value.

Financial measures are a universal expression of value: Accomplishments that can be quantified or qualified get greater respect from employers. If your student chaired a charitable fund-raiser, record how much money was raised and how its success compared to other fund-raisers. Being able to report having "raised $25,000—a fund raising record..." is more impressive than having been the fund-raising chair.

Be sure to qualify an accomplishment when it cannot be quantified. If your student received an award or recognition, be sure he or she notes the size of the candidate pool from which he or she was selected. It is impressive if ten awards were given and the total eligibility pool was ten thousand.

Learn to communicate value: Value created is value obscured if it is not communicated. People are sometimes uncomfortable talking about themselves and their accomplishments. There is a way of doing it without sounding pretentious. An annual review of your student's accomplishments is a place to start. That will make preparation for upcoming interviews easier. Here is an interview situation that can be "knocked out of the park" by those who follow our path to career survival and prosperity.

INTERVIEWER: Tell me about yourself.
RECENT GRADUATE: An interview with a company like yours is something I have looked forward to since first starting college. As a freshman I researched the kinds of skills you were looking for in entry-level candidates and worked over my four years to make sure I would be competitive...

This is an easy and impressive way to talk about accomplishments and, at the same time direct the conversation to an applicant's strengths.

H=Hear to Be Heard

There is a good chance your high school student will not be interested in talking about career management—at least not all the time. Roger Hill discovered that as he tried to engage his daughter, Veronica, in conversations about her career interest.

Out of desperation, he finally asked some of her high school teachers, "What are the kids talking about these days?" He theorized that if he found topics already of interest, his chances of communicating with Veronica would improve. That is, he took the time to hear what was on their minds so that she might eventually hear what was on his. He was surprised by what he found. A lot of the kids were talking about going to college and making sure they didn't become a dropout statistic. That is, the talk was about survival.

Students understand and are anxious to avoid becoming an undesirable statistic. It is a subject they will have heard before from peers, high school counselors, and college administrators, especially during orientation. They intuitively sense that dropping out makes the path from backpack to briefcase more difficult and is considered a negative by all concerned.

Lists of things parents and students can do to help with survival are easy to find. But it is impossible to pay attention to each and every item listed. So the question becomes what items should you pay attention to and which ones should be ignored? To find out, let's place the issue in a broader context.

That starts with clarity about the severity of the problem. Seventy percent of high school students enroll in college but only 57 percent graduate six years later. And 25 percent leave before finishing their sophomore year.

A few years ago the college completion rate in the United States led the world. Today we are twelfth as the rest of the world has caught up. Despite considerable advances, however, China and India have a long way to go before rivaling the United States in the overall quality of education provided its citizens. In that respect, comparative dropout rates matter less.

In India, for example, the quality of higher education is considered so poor that its graduates are routinely seen as unemployable. The best students leave to become educated in the United States and remain here, contributing to India's overall "brain drain."

So far the completion of one's educational journey in the United States remains a critically important personal priority rather than a national emergency—at least not yet. As a result, don't expect public policies any time soon that will address the issue.

Recall the Ford family. The cost of sending their kids to college was higher than initially planned, in part, because the kids took longer than the anticipated four years to graduate. Changes in major, a semester here and there of poor academic performance, and various other personal problems combined to drive costs up.

Parents and students are advised to do all they can to complete the journey in a timely manner. And that includes not becoming a dropout statistic. Students experience difficulties in college and drop out for many reasons, including burnout, broken relationships, lack of guidance, homesickness, drug and alcohol abuse, mental illness, life circumstances such as a death in the family, too much partying, and more.

It's almost impossible to plan for every contingency. That's why a framework that involves all interested parties in a survival partnership works best. A framework, rather than specific lists, makes it easier to pay attention to whatever is most important or relevant to your student. Most universities already have well-defined and well-rehearsed survival frameworks in place. It's up to parents and students to become familiar with on-campus resources and how they work. The partnership is depicted below.

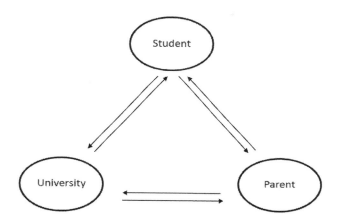

Among other things, the role of the parent is to be open, accessible, and as nonjudgmental as possible. Accusatory questions are usually not helpful in an emergency. That goes back to the previous point about saying things in ways kids can hear them. Open channels of communication improve a parent's chances of hearing about a problem in time to help prevent precipitous action.

The availability of on-campus resources is given a lot of attention during new student orientation. Be sure to ask about the university's experience with dropouts and steps they take to help prevent them. What resources are available? How does the university identify and engage students who are having difficulty or are otherwise a threat to dropping out? How do they meet their obligation to parents? Resource awareness can be a major plus. Parents and students will receive written material about these kinds of student services before the school year starts.

When a student has a preexisting condition not easily serviced by on-campus resources, make sure university officials are aware, if appropriate, and plan accordingly.

10 tips for survival

The list is intended for parents and students. They are discussion items that should be added to or deleted to fit the particulars of your situation. Ultimately students will need to carry the load.

10 Tips for
Surviving the Freshman Year in College

1. **Orientations:** Attend all orientations—especially the ones the university has identified specifically for students and/or parents. They contain valuable information and will keep you and your student from guessing where to go and what to do when an emergency arises or is anticipated.

2. **Make new friends:** Encourage your student to make new friends. That includes their roommate, class-mates, fellow club members, and other students in general. Encourage them to pal around with those who are serious and hardworking. It's a good group to get to know. The chances of finding serious, hard-working friends to pal around with are improved when you purposely look for them. Friends can also be an important safety net.

3. **Make new acquaintances:** Professors, administra-tors, and the parents of your new friends are really acquaintances rather than friends. But they can be an added plus now and later on as references or net-working contacts during your job search. College ad-ministrators in particular are easy to get to know. If your student hears an orientation presentation they particularly liked or were intrigued by, encourage them to drop the presenter a note. Tell them much they enjoyed what was presented and ask to visit dur-ing office hours for additional discussion. The pre-senter will appreciate the feedback and more than likely be willing to engage on a personal level.

4. **Use the academic advisor for advice:** Students are advised to visit their academic advisor and share

their plans for skill development. Advisors know the university's academic resources as well as anyone and can steer them to resources they may not have otherwise considered.

5. **Advise your student to get organized and remain that way:** Good organization includes getting important due dates on a calendar—exams, papers, class meetings, and other commitments. It's easier to do well when you know what you have to do and when it needs to be done. As new dates pop up, put them on the calendar.

6. **Stay healthy:** A student with healthy eating and sleeping habits will have more energy to deal with the stresses of college life. Emphasize the importance of being balanced. Greek philosophers believed balance was the key to success and a long life. Many believe they were correct.

7. **Get involved with campus life:** Not everyone is a joiner. If that describes your student, have them check out the activities of their friends and get involved through them. Remember, though, that the other side of an active campus life is the peril of becoming too busy to focus on classwork. It's about balance.

8. **Find a place to study:** The dorm room can be the absolutely worst place to study. It's difficult for a single room to provide an appropriate atmosphere for a wide range of disparate activities. Encourage them to find the right place—one conducive to concentration and getting things done. That may be the dorm room, but probably not. It probably won't be on study dates either.

9. **Revisit the placement center:** Now is a good time to revisit the placement center—this time without you. Have them find out what's coming up and what resources are available to help with the longer-term goal of developing the kind of profile employers will find attractive. It is an opportunity to put into practice what you discussed earlier.

10. **Work hard and remained focused:** Working hard at the wrong thing is not helpful. Help them stay focused on the end game—a profile that employers will find attractive.

Beyond survival

Parents help mightily when they give advice that facilitates focus. It works better when you use words and concepts your student readily understands and can use to organize their sometimes chaotic environment. That is, it is helpful if the same words and terms can be used to make decisions about courses, extracurricular activities, and social interactions that boost the development of a desirable profile. For example, it doesn't do much good to simply advise a student to "join clubs that will help later on." Much like survival, the language needs to make intuitive sense so it can be used as a guide to behavior. It is in that sense that the next suggestion is offered. Urge your student to...

Think Small: Perhaps this advice comes as a surprise. It doesn't follow the "big speech" commencement addresses that urge students to "go forth and change the world." It is also another example of how *From Backpack to Briefcase* flies in the face of conventional wisdom. The question begged is how students can add content and substance to their profiles—substance that will be attractive to employers. If your student is the type who wants to run for student body president or start another Facebook, tell them to go for it. But there is only one student body president at a time and only a few ideas that end in billionaire status. What should the rest of us try to accomplish? "Thinking small" is not a limitation on your student's ultimate destination but rather a way to ensure the success of the first few steps. It has a couple of dimensions—class size and club membership.

And they link substantively to the kind of profile employers prefer.

Small classes allow a student to get to know professors better because of more one-on-one contact. That can happen while in class, during office hours, or perhaps during social situations that develop because the contact with professors is more frequent and personable. Advise your student to make interaction with professors more than about good grades. Take it as an opportunity to learn and grow.

To decide which small classes to take, check out a professor's vitae and take a look at her research and teaching interests. And when a set of interests marries up with your student's, advise them to get to know the professor better by taking one of her small classes.

Down the line, this could open the door to opportunities for independent study, help with research, and possibly mention as a contributor on an article—tangible evidence of effective writing skills and a reference source for employers who will accept a recommendation from a professor as evidence of the ability to solve problems through research.

None of this is meant to imply that large classes are inappropriate. But students should follow a strategy that will allow more qualitative interaction with faculty. Small classes can be an effective way to go.

Once the class or research opportunity has ended, your student should stay in touch with professors by offering occasional personal updates and thanking them for the opportunity to study under their direction. Providing updates for contacts is a central tenet of social networking mentioned later.

Purposive intentions at the beginning of the college experience make it easier to remain focused. When students recognize they are in college to, among other things, get a good education or a good job, the focus is on what it takes to make that possible.

Small clubs bring a different set of possibilities into focus. Measurable results are more easily claimed as a direct result of your student's leadership, teamwork, decision-making, or problem solving and are easier to come by.

The exercise of leadership is more than being positioned as president of a club or chair of an important committee. The same is true in the development and demonstration of all the skills employers look for in recent graduates. The value comes from what is actually accomplished.

Measurable accomplishments are easier to recall, discuss, and demonstrate. It's a good idea to get a few of these under one's belt early in the college experience.

Networking: Are you serious?

Want to know a secret? Most students don't really know what networking is, or how to go about it. And a good number are frightened by the prospect of even trying. Some even see it as an inappropriate way to gain influence through contacts rather than merit. The sooner they get a different understanding, the better. But don't be in too much of a rush.

As they gain interest, explain that networking is nothing more than a way for individuals to connect with people and ideas. As students prepare for and enter the world of work, networks will be helpful in locating and connecting with people who have useful information that might otherwise be difficult to find. For example, a job seeker might be interested in who succeeds and who doesn't in certain companies in an effort to find the best culture fit. It is possible to network with people who have that information and are willing to share it.

For most young adults, networking (connecting with people) is probably not job related. People connect with one another because they are socially related or interested in the same things. It is unrealistic to expect students to network initially for purposes other than social interaction. Asking them to do so might be a big turnoff. And that includes networking for business reasons. They will eventually mature into it.

Meanwhile encourage them to be of help to others when they can. That's actually one of the fundamental tenets of networking but need not be labeled as such—at least not initially. Also encourage them to connect with people to "pick their brain." Students understand that better, and people generally like to be asked for their opinion. These are also tenets of good networking.

The point is networking has many useful components that are often best approached individually rather than included in an overall undefined concept. And it is easier to teach the concept of networking when there is a specific objective in mind. For example, before they go off to college for the first time, you could (with their approval) facilitate connecting with upperclassmen to find out what adjustments they had to make going from high school to college. Also consider asking your high school guidance office to sponsor such a program.

Many college career service centers offer noncredit courses on networking in an effort to reduce the stereotypes and fears students have about it. They too take the opportunity to define networking simply as a way of connecting with people, some of whom you know and others you just met. Eventually they will become less shy about the use of networking as a career development tool.

Internet-based social networking is a smaller part of a more significant whole. These are skills that can be learned and are not reserved only for those with outgoing personalities. Of course your student already knows how to do Internet-based social networking. But until now they may not have called it that. For him it has been tweeting, texting, or Skyping.

Getting your student from social networking to connecting for career management purposes will come with
time. Unfortunately, you will need to get their attention
before then to make sure they professionalize their online
presence and keep it that way going forward. You probably
already know why.

Inappropriate images and impressions of your student
online are forever in cyberspace available for anyone to see,
including potential employers. It's the first place they look
and is their first line of defense against bad hires.

Before social media, employers visually screened resumes to narrow the field of applicants. As the numbers of
applicants grew, they turned to software packages. Hiring
managers were still so inundated that the typical resume
submission got little more than fifteen seconds in front of
those responsible for "screening" and no time before hiring managers until later.

The hiring process continues to be time consuming and
expensive. Candidates who otherwise look fine on paper
and survive the first screen, screen themselves out if they
have inappropriate material posted online. Students learn
the hard way that indiscretions or inappropriate behavior
posted on the Internet often come back to haunt them. The
sad truth is that things already posted are in cyberspace
and difficult, if not impossible, to retrieve.

On the flip side, the freshman year is a great time to establish a professional online image by communicating with others who have similar interests. The reputation someone gains by being thoughtful and well informed can pay dividends later.

Many great websites are available for networking. Facebook and LinkedIn are strongly recommended. LinkedIn in particular is devoted to career opportunities for professionals. It has several unique features, including the ability to see who in your network is connected to others you may want an introduction to. A student may be able to contact a hiring manager well in advance of graduation. It's a good way to connect with those who may play critically important roles in the employment process.

Status updates to a network are useful at graduation because others will learn what is happening and be of assistance at a time when it's needed most. It is an effective way to venture beyond opportunities offered by the on-campus career placement center.

The freshman and sophomore years are also good times to get to know the parents of new friends and reconnect with parents you have known before. All can be excellent sources of job leads and recommendations. But they often need to be reminded of who you are and what you are looking to accomplish.

Most people are not natural networkers. Thankfully, effective use of social media does not require "social animal" status. Students already have extensive networks. It's a matter of connecting with them online for professional purposes. The freshman year is also a good time for your student to expand his or her network by connecting with new groups of friends and acquaintances through Facebook and LinkedIn.

Waiting until the senior year to develop a professionally oriented network or start a job search will likely put your student far behind others who have been proactive and more focused on their end game.

I know they can tweet, but can they communicate?

All colleges offer public speaking and writing classes. Your student should start looking into them and visit those professors ahead of when the class first meets. They should let the instructor know of their desire to take the development of communications skills seriously, to the point that it becomes a major strength by graduation. Get the instructor's ideas not only about learning to communicate more effectively but also about how to demonstrate those skills. That can lead to opportunities to publish, give presentations, and generally polish one's communications skills above and beyond most other students'.

Parents and students often wonder how a student can get published unless he or she is the second coming of Hemingway. It's easier than you think. There are plenty of opportunities to publish in local newspapers, departmental publications, online blogs, and professional meetings. You will be surprised. For example, your student might think of doing a blog article titled "Learning to Communicate More Effectively: What This College Freshman is Doing to Get Ready for a Difficult Job Market." If so, that becomes an item that will attract a lot of student comment and make an excellent addition as a bullet point on the resume.

Boomerang Kids: A Family Saga Revisited

When we last heard from John and Cynthia Ford they were struggling with John Jr.'s inability to find professional work after college. He moved home to the basement apartment, got a job walking neighborhood dogs, and began to settle into a semi-comfortable lifestyle.

The Fords were panic-stricken—another adult living in the house, student loans they might now have to service, and depleted resources for retirement. They retreated to their newly remodeled bedroom for privacy and additional planning.

We noted earlier that the rules of the new job market apply whether your student has yet to enter college, has already started, or has graduated. Regardless of where you are along the continuum, it is best to take action now. It's easier.

The Fords followed that advice and got surprisingly quick results. Here is what happened. In about a year (three months of lounging at home plus nine months of an aggressive job search), Jr. found an excellent professional job he could build a career on. Plus he still had the option of making a career change if this one did not work out. It is easier to move from one professional job to another than it is to move to a professional position from a job walking dogs, waiting tables, or tending bar.

Shortly after starting the new job, he moved out of the basement into his own reasonably priced apartment. There was enough income to live independent of Mom and Dad and begin paying down those student loans.

He briefly explored doing community service work that would have qualified him for various levels of loan forgiveness. The idea was suggested by a networking contact he first met doing volunteer work for an inner city tutoring/ mentoring program sponsored by his church. He turned the opportunity down, confident of eventually finding professional employment with enough pay to handle living expenses while meeting all other financial obligations. Teaching was not something he wanted to do long term. But the experience of networking with old contacts opened more possibilities than he knew existed.

The Fords were able to begin the long road back to financial solvency. However, none of this happened overnight or by accident. There were false starts and occasional setbacks. And it would have been easier had they started when John Jr. first went to college. But that's history. They needed to take action now. Here is a brief summary of what they did.

The end game

<u>Agreement among parents:</u> John and Cynthia knew they weren't the only parents faced with boomerang kids, but they were surprised to discover how much of an issue it was for families at all income levels throughout the country. They found Internet postings, magazine articles, and self-help groups that guided them through many of the tough issues. They also took comfort in knowing others were in the same boat and available for advice and counsel. That awareness allowed them to gather additional information before proceeding.

The first order of business was coming to a mutual understanding of their end game. Only then did they meet with Jr. to get his point of view and develop a mutually agreed on plan of action to move forward. That included a schedule of steps to be taken as well as timetables for completion.

There were surprises right from the start. For one, they discovered that they had different perspectives on the end game. Cynthia needed assurances that Jr. would not be forced out of the house prematurely. John needed to know that getting him out was a priority. Both agreed to hold off on a discussion with Jr. until they worked through differences in their respective points of view.

They also agreed to avoid one-off conversations that usually began with "Now don't tell Dad about this, but…" It was agreed that these would be met with the affirmation, "There are no secrets in this arrangement."

<u>Agreement among all concerned:</u> The meeting went well. They confirmed that Jr. wasn't happy with the living arrangement either and wanted to get out as soon as he reasonably could. But he didn't know how or when.

He described the final semester of his senior year as a whirlwind of activity with seniors all over campus in a panic to find jobs. Though a majority seemed to have found employment of some sort, there were rumors about accepting jobs that were well below expectations—jobs without health insurance; sales positions that paid 100 percent commission with no salary guarantee; and jobs with companies that had never before recruited at the university. Just as the university didn't screen students for visiting companies, they likewise were not particularly careful about screening companies for students.

Jr.'s mistakes during his initial job search became evident. Final semester of the senior year is not a good time to start looking for professional employment. It should have begun much sooner—perhaps as early as the freshman year. It also would have been helpful to have been more purposive about linking extracurricular activities to the kinds of experiences that at graduation would count for something in the eyes of employers.

<u>For everyone's mutual benefit:</u> Agreement on the end game made moving forward easier. Rather than getting him out of the house, the end game was to get Jr. on his feet—a commonality of purpose everyone could buy into. Moving out of the house would take care of itself. But just to make sure, they set a date for it to happen. What to do if the date was not met could be figured out later. With everyone on the same page, they moved forward with plans to make it happen.

<u>The same rules for everyone in the new job market:</u> Fortunately, Jr.'s standing as a recent college graduate was in place. He still had access to the campus recruiting machinery and to employers who would have relatively low expectations about previous work experience.

That's how college students tend to be viewed. That is, employers do not expect recent college graduates to have had more than one or two internships. Work experience beyond that would be viewed as an advantage over other entry-level applicants.

Jr. needed to find out as quickly as possible which employers visited campus to recruit students with his academic credentials and what other skills they were looking for. Perhaps they were still recruiting. If not, maybe a vacancy or two had occurred because a recent hire dropped out. At the very least he could introduce himself, let them know of his interest, and be considered during the next recruiting cycle. All things were possible, but he would never know until he got started.

Jr. did not have an internship during college. But he did plenty of volunteer work that could perhaps be a substitute. Maybe it was possible to get an internship now and demonstrate that he didn't just settle for a job walking neighborhood dogs.

As his job search got underway, it became clear that the resume developed during his senior year was little more than a "pie-in-the-sky" document totally disconnected from the current job market. He finally understood that his resume was not about him, but rather about what employers might want from him. His next objective was to find out what that was and be sure to give it to them during the application process.

Access to the career services center made the job search easier. Without it, however, the same steps to employment were required. He needed to find out what employers were looking for in entry-level employees and present his credentials in accordance with those requirements.

The path from where he was to where he wanted to be was bumpy and less than straightforward. And at the beginning of his journey the end was nowhere in sight. But he got started anyway and discovered that jobs were nearer at hand than he had imagined.

The situation in your family might be different from what the Fords faced. Regardless, some general rules apply that will be helpful as you deal with a family member who has boomeranged home.

Guidelines for handling boomerang kids

<u>Understand the issue:</u> The first time you get the slightest inkling that your son or daughter may move back home after college, take action. Read everything you can get your hands on to better understand the issue. It will be helpful to know whether the boomerang phenomenon is trending up or down, how it continues to be impacted by the economy, and to what extent it is being accepted as the "new normal" among this generation.

Consult campus experts to understand what they are seeing. Ask how students generally feel about living at home after graduation. How long can parents expect living at home to last?

A clearer understanding of the phenomenon will help you understand that you are not alone and others have traveled this road successfully.

<u>Get help:</u> Sometimes it's a matter of neither parent nor child knowing how to approach the issue. Taking up

residence at home after graduation could easily be something that "just happens" and no one knows how to reverse it.

At other times the situation grows out of other, even more complicated circumstances based on the needs of the child and/or the parent. This would include mental disorders, physical illnesses, and other special needs.

There is no reason to handle all situations on your own. Community-based resources are available to help, including marriage and family counseling therapy, local college and university counseling programs, and others. If you feel more comfortable getting outside help, by all means get it.

Know that people differ on the issue: None of what has been written is intended to suggest that moving home after college is an abnormality or somehow unacceptable. During a previous time in our history, multiple generations living jointly under a single roof was the norm. It was an economically efficient arrangement.

Some parents hate to see the kids leave home and would prefer that they stay. The kids may feel the same way. Find out if that is where your family is or whether you prefer to go in another direction. It is better to get those perspectives into the open.

Psychologists appear divided on the issue. At the extremes, some believe that the job of parents is to facilitate the independence of their children. Anything short of that is looked on with disfavor. Parents, the argument goes, become unwitting enablers for a lifetime of dependent children.

At the other extreme, the arrangement is viewed as a natural occurrence that harkens back to previous times and cultures when more than one generation under the same roof seemed like a logical pattern of living. The options are yours to choose.

More adults in the house: Having another adult in the house poses special challenges. It's more expensive generally for parents and less convenient for all concerned. Keeping the peace requires that the issues are identified and dealt with. Who has what responsibilities and when? Is Mom expected to cook and clean perhaps as she did before? Who pays the car insurance? Can everyone come and go as they please as if living in a hotel? Are family members obligated to say where they are going and when they expect to return?

Though you may not have these particular issues, there will be others. Create a mechanism for getting them surfaced as well as a forum for discussion and resolution. Don't wait until the pot is boiling to understand that more than two adults in the house is different from what has gone before or from what was expected. It requires coordination and effective communication. Get started now.

These issues are complicated when your adult student includes a dependent child and/or a spouse or significant other. Including outside family members may require special finesse. The situations are too numerous to delineate here. Understand that unexpected issues that require attention can and will arise. Be prepared to give them whatever attention they need.

Find your end game: It should be easy to see why it is important to clarify what you want to accomplish. It becomes the yardstick by which all actions are measured. It is also your compass for determining when you are off course.

The interpersonal relations that invariably accompany intergenerational issues are tricky and complex. Having an end game that can be shared with others helps to simplify and facilitate discussion.

Until now your child has been allowed to treat your home as if it were his own. The idea that your child should exit and is not free to return at will without prior negotiation may require some getting used to. At some time parents may have insisted, "This will always be your home, no matter what happens."

An end game that seeks to have the child exit and build his or her own independent life may require some getting used to—maybe not. But don't assume everyone understands and agrees with your end game.

Find your child's end game: Your next step is to understand your child's expectations. There is a very good chance they are the same as yours. Kids generally want their own place with the freedom to do as they please without interference from Mom and Dad. But don't assume that.

Living at home for some period of time can be an attractive option. It is easier to save money while living a comfortable lifestyle. Some kids even see living at home after graduation as a favor to their parents. Perhaps you see it this way as well. Be sure to ask your child about his or her end game and do not assume you already know what it is.

Time limits: If the expectation is that the child will eventually move out, it is important to set a time limit for it to happen. It's the same reasoning we used initially to have a discussion about attending college. Once they draw the connection between college and professional work, it becomes easier to develop plans that lead in that direction. Without specific goals and occasional reminders, students tend to lose focus and busy themselves with other things.

Time limits are recommended for the same reason. Establishing a "move-out" date allows for a similar kind of planning around the steps necessary to make moving out possible. It helps focus attention on things such as conducting a job search, saving money, etc.

Rent or no rent: Needless to say, parents are conflicted. According to some estimates, about half of all boomerang kids pay rent. Here are some reasons why you may want to consider it.

Expense: Another adult in the house is more expensive than it would otherwise be. Additional costs include food, utilities, wear and tear, car insurance, and even additional cable channels you would not have subscribed to. Rent may be a matter of fairness and affordability.

Too cushy: You may not want to make it so cushy that they never leave. It's akin to having one's cake and eating it too. If they get too comfortable, the incentives are aligned for them to stay.

Forced savings: Kids live at home to save money. Otherwise they might not have the first and last months' rent to secure an apartment, a deposit to get the utilities in their name, or to furnish the apartment appropriately. Parents sometimes quietly set the rent aside and later return it when the child is about to move out.

Rent may also help prevent taking on debt that could extend your student's stay at home. A new automobile, cell phone, computer, and associated monthly expenses add up, making moving more difficult. Forced savings could be a solution.

Clear communications: Now is a good time to revisit two of the rules we mentioned as necessary for effective communication with your teen. The most obvious difference between then and now is that the journey to adulthood has largely been completed. Though they may need you less, important contributions remain to be made.

We need to amend the advice we gave to "deal with things that are important to them." Those discussions were about them, not about you. Our advice now is to deal with things that are important to both of you. It's time to get your oar in the water in a different way. It's your house, retirement security, and lifestyle that may be at stake. It's them learning how to live independent of Mom and Dad, if that was what was agreed to.

That being said, you still need to talk in a way so they will listen and listen in a way so they will talk. It is a basic tenet of all communications. Keep it in play.

<u>Agree to discuss:</u> These can be sensitive subjects during difficult times. As such, discussion may not come easy. You will likely get feedback in the form of "Do we really have to talk about this again?" Strike an agreement at the very beginning of the discussions to do a check-in at regular intervals. Acknowledge that the discussions may be difficult and that neither of you will necessarily feel like having them. But get agreement to have them anyway. It will keep frustrations from building and suddenly exploding.

Epilogue

Late Bloomers, et al.

I learned a thing or two about late bloomers from Malcolm Gladwell's article on the subject in the October 20, 2008, issue of the *New Yorker*. Until then I had not given them much thought. In retrospect that is surprising and disappointing.

Gladwell wrote about Ben Fountain's sudden explosion onto the American literary scene with the publication in 2006 of *Brief Encounters with Che Guevara*. "The reviews," wrote Gladwell, "were sensational. It won awards and drew comparisons to Graham Greene, Evelyn Waugh, Robert Stone, and John le Carré."[30] But Fountain's ascent wasn't sudden at all. Truth was he gave up the practice of law to toil away at writing for eighteen long years before hitting it big. Prior to having penned a best seller he would have perhaps been best known as a stay-at-home dad—one supported by a hardworking wife so he could amuse himself in what might have turned out to have been a self-indulgent pipe dream. Fountain quit his job at age thirty and came out the other side eighteen years later at forty-eight with a best-selling book. As such, he qualifies as a genuine late bloomer.

Several famous late bloomers are mentioned, including the great postimpressionist painter Paul Cézanne (1839-1906) who turned away from law against his father's wishes at age twenty-two. During the early years, it looked as if his dad may have had a point because recognition as an artist came neither easy nor early. Cézanne was famously criticized for an inability to draw, was known to quit on works he spent months and even years developing, and was notorious for slashing partially finished canvases in disgust. Others around him, including his father, continued their support. They never allowed Cézanne to confuse struggle with failure. What qualifies him as a late bloomer? He didn't have his own one-man show until age fifty-six, and works he completed later in life are generally more highly valued than earlier ones. For example, in 2011, Cézanne's "Les Pommes" sold at auction for $41.6 million—a painting he started at age fifty. "Let's just be thankful," commented Gladwell, "that Cézanne didn't have a guidance counselor in high school who looked at his primitive sketches and told him to try accounting."

Since reading Gladwell's article I've paid more attention to the varying lengths of time it takes before people hit their stride. It simply takes some a lot longer than others. But what can we do with that information? Does it help us provide guidance and counseling to our kids?

I have also wondered why the idea of being a late bloomer isn't routinely accounted for in the way kids are counseled. Maybe it is, but I doubt it. In fact, the feedback kids get seems to be encapsulated within an artificially imposed timetable. Those who graduate high school, college, and perhaps graduate school on or ahead of schedule are said to be doing well. Though they may never reach the level of Fountain or Cézanne, they are treated more like prodigies in that they are easy to recognize and deal with.

How we counsel kids is embedded in an educational calendar derived in part from a need to plan and coordinate at the local, state, and national levels. To accomplish this we use broad-based socioeconomic data that in turn have implications for how we think about our children's progress.

Those who stray from generally accepted timetables, or whose ceiling may be lower than others, are more difficult. We can only see who they are and whether they are worth the investment after the fact. The term "worth the investment" is offered tongue-in-cheek. The purpose of the epilogue is to suggest that if you don't invest in your children regardless of how far in life someone predicts they can go few others will either. And that is especially true when your investment is based more on a leap of faith than on concrete evidence they will succeed.

Maya Angelou got off to a rough start in life and was mute from ages eight to thirteen. Her eventual success could not have been predicted. Yet she became widely recognized for countless contributions to society mainly through her poetry. She won numerous awards including a Grammy, the Mother Teresa Award, and the Presidential Medal of Freedom, the Nation's highest civilian honor.

J.K. Rowling also comes to mind. Who among us could have predicted that as a single mother on public assistance she would become the most successful author the world has even known? Susan Boyle is another. She became an internationally acclaimed singing star at age forty-eight. Her explanation as to why she was so late coming to the profession was that she had never before been given the opportunity.

I am particularly attracted to the word "opportunity" for late bloomers as well as for others. Who knows what you will find in your kids when they are given an opportunity.

I also learned a thing or two from my son Todd last year as we sat observing his son come down a water slide time and time again with more respect and caution than the incline deserved. Much younger kids slid down with a lot more abandon than Sebastian.

"I wish he showed more daring."

"Yes, I do too," Todd commented, "but that's our problem, not his. Let's make sure we keep it that way."

I was both startled and pleased by my son's insight and wisdom. Sebastian and all our grandchildren will do okay in life because it's something they will largely determine for themselves. But their level of family support will not depend on how quickly they come down the slide or ascend the educational ladder. They will go as far as their personal platform, willingness to work hard, and focus will take them. Our job is to help develop as much of those as we possibly can.

When I first got the idea for this book, I was invited to speak to a group of union employees in the Montgomery County, Maryland, Parks Department. These were hourly workers, most of whom had little or no college. My first thought was that the book I was about to write did not apply. It is disappointing not to have known better. The more I have studied the new job market the more I have come to understand that its rules apply to all, whether someone has a GED or PhD. The name of the game is called contribution. Those who learn how to contribute get further ahead. But who knows how far that will be?

Take the case of Jhaqueil Reagan, whose human-interest story went viral on February 26, 2013. The headline read "Teen Hikes 10 Miles to Interview in Snow Storm." "Jhaqueil Reagan, an Indianapolis teen, set out to walk 10 miles in the freezing cold to a job interview before he was picked up by a complete stranger and given a job on the spot, no questions asked."

Here is what happened. On the way he stopped outside a local restaurant for directions and was told his destination was six to seven miles ahead. He was also advised to take a bus because the weather was bad and perhaps getting worse. Jhaqueil simply thanked the stranger and kept walking.

Their paths crossed again a few miles farther as Art Bouvier and his wife were on their way to a coffee shop and recognized Reagan from a few miles before. They stopped and offered a ride, which was accepted.

On the way they talked about where he was headed and why he was walking. As it turns out, Jhaqueil was headed to an interview for a minimum wage ($7.25/hr.) job at Dairy Queen. He was walking because he could not afford to do otherwise. Reagan explained that his mother had died of cancer two years earlier, forcing him to drop out of school and get a job to help care for his siblings. Having just finished his GED, he was now looking for other employment.

The restaurant where they first met is called Papa Roux and is owned by the man who was now giving him a ride. Bouvier offered him a job on the spot with no questions asked and at twice the minimum wage. The story was initially positioned as a "Tale of a Good Samaritan." It was really an act born of self-interest.

Finding in-store help like Jhaqueil Reagan is difficult. Bouvier had learned to recognize people who might contribute to his business and refused to let the opportunity pass. Jhaqueil obviously possessed two of the three characteristics that would predict he could make a positive contribution—a willingness to work hard and the ability to focus. An eighteen-year-old focused on a worthy mission with a willingness to work however hard he needed to get it accomplished is easily worth the risk of a job offer.

I don't know how high Jhaqueil's ceiling is. How far can someone with "only" a GED with his personal platform really ascend? He can certainly go farther than some might predict. I offer as evidence that his first job search out of the gate netted a position at twice what he was asking.

While putting the finishing touches on this book, I came across an article written by George Will titled "Jon Will's Gift." I had the pleasure of working under Will while earning my doctorate from Michigan State University. That's where I learned that the soundness and value of my point of view was in the process used to arrive at my conclusions and not in my political predisposition. It's disappointing that I haven't paid more attention to what I had previously learned.

Jon, George's son, was born with Down syndrome. But it hasn't kept George from being a proud papa. On May 4, 2012, Jon was the subject of his father's column in the *Washington Post*. It was John's fortieth birthday—an important milestone given that at the time of his birth, life expectancy of Down syndrome babies was about twenty years. The Will family was given the option of leaving Jon and the care he would require for others to attend to for the balance of Jon's life. "In 1972, people with Down syndrome were commonly called Mongoloids. Now they are called American citizens...and their life expectancy is 60." George Will's column is useful and harkens back to my graduate school days under his tutelage. From the beginning, Will concerned himself with his responsibilities as a parent and not with the limitations Jon brought or did not bring at birth. In this sense he was a perfect helicopter parent. He gave Jon an opportunity and Jon, in his own way, was able to run with it. He didn't allow the level of his support to be dictated by societal norms, nor did he fret because Jon's ceiling was different from his. Opportunity was what was needed and opportunity was what Jon got.

When your kids fail to gain admission to as good a school as you want—when they choose a college major that you think doesn't optimize future career choices—or when they boomerang back home because they cannot afford to do otherwise, remember, their journey has just begun.

Their life expectancy will extend upward toward ninety years. Don't let your disappointment become their problem and don't confuse struggle with failure. There are lots of people who overcome a "rough" start especially when given an opportunity. Some of them will even turn out to be late bloomers.

Appendix #1

Ways to Pay for College

My good friend and colleague Dr. Pam Rambo, owner of Rambo Research and Consulting (http://www.ramboresearch-andconsulting.com), shows her clients how to pay for college using other people's money. She gets a lot of attention because it is the kind of help people need and appreciate. My comments are intended to help you take the first step toward making college affordable.

There are four basic sources of funds to pay for college: personal savings, grants/scholarships, loans, and work-study. Important and sometimes complicated nuances exist within each of those categories, so be sure to start your research as early as possible. Visit your student's local high school guidance counselor or a college financial aid office. They will have enough information to keep you busy for quite a while.

You will also find it helpful to estimate what it will cost for your student to attend his or her college(s) of choice. That's fairly easy to accomplish because all colleges are federally mandated to provide online calculators to help estimate the cost.

GRANTS

These are sometimes called "gift aid" because they do not have to be paid back. They are offered by various organizations, including local, state, and federal governments, foundations, companies, private individuals, and community-based groups. High school guidance counselors and the Internet are excellent sources of information.

The most widely used monies of this type are Pell grants from the federal government administered by the US Department of Education. Founded during the Nixon administration as Basic Educational Opportunity Grants (BEOG), they are based on the assessed needs of students and awarded on the basis of merit.

Designed originally as financial support for low-income families, they have come under political attack and today cover much less of the cost of a four-year education. Some circumstances, such as withdrawing from school, trigger a requirement to repay the grant.

Other types of grants include Federal Supplemental Educational Opportunity Grants (FSEOG), Teacher Educational Assistance for College & Higher Education (TEACH), and grants awarded to armed services personnel who served in Iraq and Afghanistan. Again, information is readily available.

SCHOLARSHIPS

Scholarships are also merit-based awards, aimed at particular groups and sponsored by a variety of sources including all levels of government, private industry, foundations, and private individuals. There are thousands of scholarships available, though many go begging every year. The US Department of Labor has a free scholarship search tool available. Also consult the reference section of any library, state and federal agencies, the financial aid office of most colleges and universities, and your student's high school career guidance office.

SAVINGS

An early start to a college savings program provides more opportunity to fund college without additional strain on the family budget. As the cost of college rose, various local, state, and federal agencies gave additional support to tax-effective savings programs to make college more affordable. The leader among these are 529 plans, so called because they are named after section 529 of the IRS code and administered by state agencies and organizations.

The College Savings Plan Network (CSPN) is the national coordinating body affiliated with the National Association of State Treasurers. 529s are an effective way of shielding dedicated educational monies and their returns from taxation. There are restrictions and differences. Knowing the facts and making choices based on your individual requirements is important. Under some plans it is possible to shift the money from one recipient to another, freeze the cost of tuition to insulate families from a portion of future tuition hikes, and many other positive features. Consult the CSPN website for additional detail and a state-by-state comparison of plans.

STUDENT LOANS

The easy advice is "don't borrow to pay for college." But that may not be possible. Further, borrowing low-interest-rate monies to pay for college expenses may be a desirable alternative. But taking on heavy debt without a plan to navigate the path to career survival and prosperity is risky. Anyone who wants to attend college can do so because there are a variety of loan options available.

Subsidized Federal Loans: They are needs based and subsidized in the sense that the federal government pays the interest while the student is enrolled. They are also regulated, long term (ten-year standard payback period) with low interest rates. The monies are dispersed through lending institutions (banks and credit unions) or the federal government itself. Forgiveness and deferment are possible and worth looking into.

Unsubsidized Federal Loans/ Stafford Loans: These are also long-term, low-interest loans. The interest is the responsibility of the borrower, but repayment can be deferred until graduation.

Federal Plus Loans: These are loans for parents to help defray the cost of their children's college expenses. Based on credit history, they are also low-interest-rate loans, and repayment begins sixty to ninety days after graduation.

Federal Perkins Loans: Based on extreme financial need with interest rates lower than other federally available loans.

Private Lenders: Financing a college education is sufficiently lucrative to attract private lenders. The programs vary, may not be forgivable, but most are long-term loans.

WORK-STUDY

Parents understand the importance of good grades and often prefer that their students don't work. They believe the more time students are free to study the better. I encourage you to rethink the assumption. College offers students more free time than many have ever previously experienced. Suddenly they are required to structure their days and weeks as never before. Regular hours imposed by a work schedule could be a blessing. Though the evidence in support of this idea is anecdotal, it deserves consideration.

Work-study programs are usually on-campus jobs available to students on a part-time basis to help defray expenses. Federally funded work-study (FWS) programs are needs based and require an application and supporting documentation. If your student fails to qualify based on need for FWS, apply for nonfunded work-study (NFWS) positions. Both are available depending on the availability of funds. The information provided on funding a college education is just enough to get you started. Be sure to choose your most cost-effective funding options. They are not necessarily the most visible or the first to come to your attention.

Planning is required to gather the funds for college. It's an expensive investment that deserves a well thought out end game. Getting into college and working out a funding package is such a relief that you and your student may want to relax and enjoy the moment. Now is the wrong time to relax. Concentrate on the path forward.

Appendix #2

Traditionally Underserved Kids

African Americans and Hispanics are two significant populations whose income levels have been disproportionately skewed toward the bottom. To correct this imbalance, a concerted effort has been made to provide access to higher education—the same escalator that has traditionally supported upward mobility across the board. Dramatic increases in enrollments have taken place from the 1960s beginning with African Americans and then Hispanics. According to the National Center for Education Statistics, black enrollment as a percentage of the total enrollment rose from under 5 percent in 1968 to 14.3 percent by the year 2010. Hispanics have gone from under 3 percent to 12.5 percent in the same time frame, with dramatic increases as of late.

Much of the enrollment increases have occurred in for-profit institutions. Minorities are aggressively recruited with promises of "a good job and better life through education"—not unlike the recruitment practices of not-for-profit schools. One big difference is the lack of admission requirements and subsequent reliance on federal aid (Pell grants and other federally insured loans). Scheduling flexibility provided by 24/7 online access works especially well for students with full- or part-time jobs. It also works for military personnel located around the world.

Whether for-profits are great service providers or exploiters is being actively debated. Students at for-profit institutions account for 12 percent of all students, 23 percent of all federal aid, and nearly half of all student loan defaults. The students enter college less academically prepared and do not fare well in the new job market. Though for-profit colleges promise an education that will lead to jobs, they provide little evidence that suggests they deliver any better than others. Just the opposite may be true.

Traditionally underserved populations have clearly brought into the "go to college, get a job" ethos. They and their parents could be bitterly disappointed to discover a job market that has changed its collective mind about the value of their college credential. There needs to be an all-out effort to get the word out to these communities that the degree by itself is no longer sufficient and that what is accomplished while in school is as important as the degree itself.

The Great Recession hit these populations particularly hard. According to a July 2011 Pew report, the median wealth of white households was twenty and eighteen times that of black households and Hispanic households respectively, the largest gap since the government started publishing this data more than twenty-five years ago.

Further, 24 percent of black and Hispanic households were reported to have zero assets other than a vehicle as compared with just 6 percent of white households. As greater numbers of blacks and Hispanics attend college, well-paying jobs at graduation take on added meaning. Members of some groups may now hesitate to "bet the farm" on the earning power of today's college diploma. Others, thanks to the Great Recession, do not have a farm to bet.

Appendix #3

The For-Profit Controversy

Let's take a moment to better understand the controversy surrounding for-profit schools and why you should pay attention. For-profit schools cater particularly to part-time students, many of whom work full time and need the 24/7 online access to courses, a method of teaching used by many educational institutions but particularly favored by for-profits. The controversy comes because they often do not have admission requirements (anybody can get in) and recruit students more aggressively than many of their not-for-profit counterparts.

Though motivated by educational concerns, they are often accused of being motivated primarily by profit. They have been the fastest-growing segment of higher education over the past fifteen years with an enrollment of more than 2.4 million students. Their rise in popularity in this era of college as a private benefit rather than a public good is understandable. It is a way for students who may not otherwise qualify for admission to gain access to the upward mobility escalator college has become.

Their method of enrolling and financing students is a major source of the controversy. A recent study of thirty of the largest for-profit universities concluded that they admit students and charge exorbitant tuition fees paid for by federally funded programs. Many students are thought to be otherwise unprepared for college. In the main, students attending for-profit universities borrow more and graduate less by several magnitudes.

What has any of this got to do with you as a student or parent? Perhaps you have seen, read, or heard advertisements that promise a financially secure life for graduates from for-profit universities. These promises are the same as those made by the traditional not-for-profit institutions. The truth is "go to college, get a job, and join the middle class" is less possible for graduates of all types of institutions. If you are considering a for-profit school, parents are advised to be doubly attentive because they have not adequately addressed the issues either.

What difference does it make? Until higher education in general addresses the issues more aggressively, graduates of for-profit schools are left with credentials that do not carry equivalent weight in the job market.

Martha was a recent associate's degree graduate from a local for-profit college. As a single mother of two, she needed a good-paying job ASAP, and she got one by developing an edge in the job market. It came when she made sure during her internship assignment that no other intern outworked or outperformed her. She was always on time, cooperative, friendly, and did whatever needed doing. And she did it with distinction. Patients routinely commented on her ability to make them feel welcomed and comfortable.

She got the only job offer available to fifteen competing interns. It wasn't easy, but Martha found the extra that Tom Friedman talked about. It is what your student may need to do as well.

(Endnotes)

[1] (http://ca.finance.yahoo.com/blogs/pay-day-/boomerang-kid)

[2] http://www.huffingtonpost.com/2013/09/30/student-loans-default_n_4019806.html

[3] (http://www.insidehighered.com/views/2013/10/17/liberal-arts-are-best-preparation-even-business-career-essay)

[4] http://money.cnn.com/magazines/fortune/fortunearchive/1966/04/01/210981/

[5] (http://www.timesuniion.com/business/article/IBMlayoffs-a-sign-of-flux-4675842.php.)

[6] (http://jobs.aol.com/articles/2011/12/07/the-biggest-corporate-layoffs-of-all time/

[7] (http://usatoday30.usatoday.com/money/workplace/2003-08-05-outsourcing_x.htm)

[8] Reid Hoffman and Ben Casnocha, The Start Up of You: Adapt to the Future, Invest in Yourself, and Transform Your Career: (Crown Publishing, 2012)

[9] (http://www.insidehighered.com/news/2014/02/20/private-bridge-programs-expand-fill-college-career-gap)

[10] (http://www.maketplace.org/topics/business/fallout-financial-crisis/why-more-engineers-are-losing-jobs)

[11] (see, "Take it from an Ex-journalist: Adapt of Die" in The Chronicle of Higher Education http://chronicle.texterity.com/chronicle/20130927a?subid=NintWPfoGudF#pg1).

[12] (http://www.pewresearch.org/daily-number/most-parents-expect-their-children-to-attend-college/)

[13] (http://www.nbcnews.com/id/10154383/ns/business-personal finance/t/college-freshmen-face-major-dilemma/)

[14] (http://online.wsj.com/article/5810001424052748704554 10575435563989873060.html?mod=wsj_PathToProfessors-TopLEADNewsCollection)

[15] (http://.huffingtonpost.com/2012/08/15/cost-of-college-degree-increase-12-fold-1120-percent-bloomberg_n_1783700.html

[16] (http://www.dailyastorian.com/opinion/editorials/editorial-the-disappearing-summer-job/article_53d47296-d448-11e2-9f49-001a4bcf887a.html)

[17] Adele Faber and Elaine Mazlish, How to Talk So Kids will Listen & Listen So Kids Will Talk: (New York: Avon Books, Inc., 1999)

[18] (http://latimesblogs.latimes.com/money_co/2011/08/college-gradutates-pay.html)

[19] (http://www.coloradoan.com/article/20130829/COLUMNISTS91/308290038)

[20] (http://www.nytimes.com/2012/01/25/opinion/friedman-average-is-over.html)

[21] Richard Arum and Josipa Roksa, Academically Adrift: Limited Learning On College Campuses: (Chicago, University of Chicago Press, 2011)

22 http://www.nytimes.com/2011/01/09/education/
edlife/09books-t.html?_r=0

23 Steven D. Levitt and Stephen J. Dubner, Freakonomics: A
rogue Economist Explores the Hidden Side of Everything:
(New York: William Marrow, 2005) p. 175

24 (http://www.brookings.edu/~/media/research/files/
reports/2008/2/economic%20mobility%20sawhill/02_
economic_mobility_sawhill_ch1.pdf

25 (http://www.brookings.edu/research/papers/2007/11/
generations-isaacs)

26 (http://qz.com/155397/americans-who-say-college-
isnt-for-everyone-never-mean-their-own-kids/)

27 (http://online.wsj.com/public/resources/documents/
info-Degrees_that_Pay_you_Back-sort.htm)

28 (http://money.cnn.com/magazines/fortune/
fortunearchive/1966/04/01/210981/)

[29] (http://www.nytimes.com/2014/02/23/opinion/sunday/friedman-how-to-get-a-job-at-google.html?action=click&contentCollection=Opinion&module=MostEmailed&version=Full&region=Marginalia&src=me&pgtype=article)

[30] (http://www.newyorker.com/reporting/2008/10/20/081020fa_fact_gladwell?currentPage=all)

Index

Academic and career success, 35, 65-73

academically adrift, 45, 47, 52, 70, 72

Academically Adrift: Limited Learning n College Campuses (*Arum and Roksa*), 70

accusations, unintended, 61

African Americans, 9, 163

Alice in Wonderland, 84

American Pubic Media marketplace, 33

Angelou, Angela, 150

Annenberg Institute for School Reform, 78

anxiously employed, 37

Arum, Richard with Josipa Roksa, (*Academically Adrift: Limited Learning on College Campuses*), 70

"average is over," 68-9

boomerang kids, 4, 13, 18, 133-45

Boyle, Susan, 150

brain drain, India, 117

Brief Encounters with Che Guevara, 147

Bronfman, Edgar, 15

Brookings Institute, 75-6

Brooks, Kate, 94

Brown University, 78

campus career services, 30, 34-5, 49-54, 56, 59, 61, 87, 115, 138

campus clubs, importance of, 112-13

Casnocha, Ben, 19

career counseling, 31-33, 59, 60-64, 98, 149

career services, 30, 34, 48, 50, 54, 56-58, 61, 87-101, 105, 138

Cezanne, Paul, 148

China, 13, 19, 117

choosing the right college, 55

choosing the right major, 30,51, 52

Chronicle of Higher Education, 33

college administrators, 24, 26, 28, 47, 68, 73, 88-89, 92, 95, 117, 121

college as a four year job search, 87-113

college athletic coaches, 83

college cost, 2, 11, 13, 34, 55, 57, 66, 68, 118, 158, 160

college degree, value of, 2, 10, 16

college faculty, 24, 26, 28, 33, 34, 47, 66, 70, 73, 83, 88, 93, 95-96, 125

college graduates, recent, 3, 14

college majors, 15

college presidents,32

college, saving for, 10, 33, 76, 83-85

college to career, linkages, 43, 48

command and control, 35

corporate lay-offs, 14, 90

cost of college 10-14, 22, 32, 38-39, 64, 84-86, 91

down syndrome, 154

Dubner, Stephen, 74

Ehrenreich, Barbara, 37

engineering graduates, 21, 40, 45, 105, 111

externships, 100

Facebook, 124, 130

Farber, Adele, 39

focus, 26, 29, 68, 73, 79-80, 84-86, 123, 126, 131, 143, 151, 153

for-profit universities, 3, 4, 13, 164, 167-169

Fountain, Ben, 147

Freakonomics: A Rogue Economist Explores The Hidden Side Of Everything (Leavitt & Dubner), 74

Friedman, Tom, 68, 169

Georgetown University, 66

Gladwell, Malcolm, 147-148

good jobs, 48

Google, 110

Grandparents, 23

grants-in-aid, 157, 164

Grasgreen, Ellie, 20

Great Recession, 12, 72, 165

Half, Robert, 42

Hall, Barbara, 36

hard work, 81-84

Hoffman, Reid, 19

Highpoint University, 93-94

high school seniors

Huffington Post, 14

IBM, 16-18

India, 13, 18, 116

Inside Higher Education, 20
intergenerational mobility,
74-80
internship programs, 20, 50, 52,
54, 57, 100, 112-113, 137

job market, 1, 6, 12-29, 36, 58,
65-86
job security, 13, 145

lay-offs, 17-18
Les Pommes, 148
liberal arts majors, 15, 24, 96
LinkedIn, 18, 130

Madison Square Garden, 19
mba, cost of hiring India v.
USA, 19
mba programs, 98
McDonalds, 9
Michigan State University, 153
Montgomery County, Maryland
Parks Dept., 151
mutual expectations, 59, 136-137

National Association of Colleges
and Employers (NACE), 24,
44, 94
National Center for Educational
Statistics, 163
Networking, 101, 126-130, 134
new student orientation, 84, 91,
93, 117-118, 120

New York Times, 74
New Yorker Magazine, 147
Northwestern University, 97

occupational downgrade, 21
Ohio State University, The, 97

parent involvement
parent-student partnership
parting ceremonies, 91
parents
   boomerang kids, 13, 18,
      133-144, 154
   counseling your student,
      30, 33, 59, 60-64, 98,
      140, 149
   helicopter, 26, 92, 154
   is your career center up to
      snuff, 98, 99-103
   meeting with career center
      director, 92, 110, 106-108
   overview—what parents need
      to know, 9-34
   skill development tips, 113-115
   skills your student needs, 15,
      53, 60, 67-68, 70, 72, 80, 81,
      88 92, 94, 96, 102-110, 125,
      126, 128, 131, 137
   talk with your student, how to,
      43-55
Pell Grants, 158, 164
Pennsylvania State University, 31
placement center, 88, 123, 130

Rambo Research and consulting, 4-5, 157
Reagan, Jhaquiel, 151-152
Roksa, Josipa with Richard Arum (*Academically Adrift: Limited Learning On College Campuses*), 70-71
Romans, Angela, 78
Rowling, JK, 150

Scholarships, 157, 159
Silicon Valley, 19, 108
skill development, 108-115, 121, 126, 131
skills
    communication, 38-40, 59, 70, 72, 94, 101, 108, 112, 131, 141, 145
    decision-making, 43, 65, 74, 109, 111, 126
    honesty and integrity, 110
    leadership, 67, 94, 109, 111, 126
    listening, 38-39, 48
    problem solving, 110-111, 125-126
small classes, importance of, 124-126

social media, 126-130
student debt, 10-15, 66-67, 72, 144, 160
student loans, 10, 14, 106, 133-134, 157, 160-161, 164
summer jobs, 36
survival tips, college, 116-119, 120-127

technical skills, 15-16, 67, 80, 110
Texas A & M, 31
The Start Up of You: Adapt to the future: Invest in Yourself: and Transform Your Career (Reid Hoffman and Ben Casnocha), 19

underemployed, 37
United States, 116-118
University of Illinois, 31
University of Pennsylvania, 97
University of Vermont, 91

Wake forest University, 94
Wall Street Journal, 31, 82
Will, George, 153-154
Will, Jon, 153-154
work study, 157, 161-162

34562069R00106

Made in the USA
San Bernardino, CA
03 May 2019